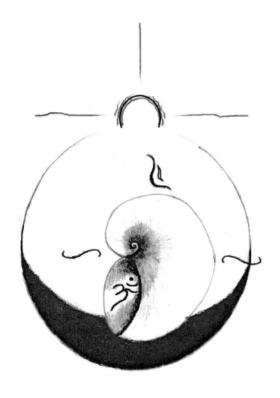

A Rhapsody of Art Creation

The Archer

Songs of Yama

Joseph Montgomery

ISBN: 978-1508512516

First published in the United States by createspace.com.
www.createspace.com

Joseph Montgomery

Indie Published Works:

Temple: A Collection of Ecstatic Poetry

Kentucky: Ecstatic Grassroots

- Available on Amazon

Social Media:

RhapsodyofArt.com
Rhapsody of Art on Facebook

Contact:

RhapsodyofArt@gmail.com

Introduction

There is a saying in the village-tongue of a far-away culture, spoken with high reverence, every child is taught its meaning— and upon initiation into marriage and manhood, they begin the path of understanding that meaning.

The adage is called: Depoah Manu— "The Love that kills..."

Every lover experiences this phenomenon, removing the ego in order to move them from the limitations of their love into the expanded experience of one's own Being.

In this book, Yama and Kathrana find themselves both outcasts from the conditions of their culture, with a sense of homelessness, they have found each other...

Now they find themselves on the road of Depoah Manu... Yama reckons with his ecstasy through Ecstatic poetry, meanwhile, telling the tale of his relationship with Kathrana, a journey that will teach them both how to die.

If you don't take the time
to discover who you are

no one will ever meet you

where you long to be seen.

A Story in Love

Yama sat under the bend of trees, their branches leaning over the light of his fire, a fresh load of wood singing inside the flames. His eyes were deeply set inside the wists of orange— his mind lost inside the dance.

He didn't realize it, but his fingers were stroking the cordage of his bow, dark fingernails sliding across the taught string. His gear was set aside and dinner had recently been prepared. A bowl of soy-paste and rice. The spoon sat unused in the bowl. He couldn't bring himself to eat.

How far would they be willing to hunt me? He thought. *Not further than the River...* he looked at his hands. *They wouldn't have anything to bring back... I would die before they have me.*

Yama's eyes suddenly quickened. His hands gripped the wood of his bow.

Standing to his feet he lay his weapon down and looked up through a gap in the canopy. A sky polluted with light lay beyond the opening, a single star beaming through the low illumined haze of a distant city, The Empire of Light— The star jingled there above him, a dull bulb hanging through the roughage of the treetops, and he felt it was mocking him.

He looked around at the night that surrounded, broken only by the swishing of his fire through low gusts of wind. "Nights of Mystery!" he sounded through the silence. "Are you not the source of the unspoken? Do you see what my heart is saying now? Bring me love! I will die another day without it. Bring me love, Oh night, bring me beauty, so the war may end in me."

Suddenly, upon Yama's arm landed a Moth out of the shadows. It appeared to him like a couplet of maple leaves for wings, with ferns upon his head as antennae, and a soft figure, like the buds of a Spring bloom. Yama was captivated. With his hand he caught the creature and lifted it to his lips to kiss it— at that moment the creature's beauty faded. It fell from his lips and lifted like ash, slain by the kiss. Then the remains, trembling inside his hands, transforming into moonlight.

He dropped the small bulb of soft light to the ground and stepped back, looking around him into the shadows wicking closer to his camp— the moonlight of the beautiful creature was glowing upward onto his legs.

""Nights of Mystery! You are playing me? Are you not the depth of knowing? Are you blind to the suffering of my heart? So bring me love! I will die another day without it. Bring me love, Oh night, bring me beauty, so the war may end in me."

So, out of the trees came another Moth. It appeared to him like a lotus flower with wings which seemed to blossom, full and dense, upon its soft back. Upon its head were antennae of silver and the body glimmered with the dew of morning.

The Moth came to Yama's shoulder, and he, so admiring the beauty of the creature, caught it inside his fingers and kissed it upon the wings. And again, as the moth before it had done, the creature fell slain into his palm and became moonlight in his hands...

A great shadow suddenly leapt off Yama's back, firelight shifting, he called toward the darkness with the very most of his voice, demanding: "Are you the void that listens, or aren't you? If I truly cannot kiss the beautiful with my own lips, or touch love with this mouth, without slaying them dead— than I would rather give this kiss to myself."

And so, upon Yama's arm crept a spider, a black widow, crawling on eight thin needles of black, dragging its body like bulbs of coal, as wicked as spite and a red-hot hourglass upon its abdomen. Yama lifted his elbow, and after a breath, kissed the spider—the creature returned to Yama a kiss of her own.

A women then appeared in place of the spider and spoke in a gentle voice: "Soldier, that kiss has poisoned you. You will suffer now, before death."

The woman, known as the Daughter of the Moon, stood before Yama, as full and delicate as a white valley of snow. Pale shoulders showed themselves like the hills of a countryside, her neck a pink clay river... She carried herself with seduction, but with a knowing in her eyes that assured, she herself was not seduced. She was perfection for every man, according to their taste, according to the dream in their mind— any man who looked upon her, invited the danger of complete, inseparable enchantment.

Daughter of the Moon noticed Yama's mossy green eyes were hiding from her- "What are you afraid to see, Yama, son of Dapha?'

"I've been to many places," he said with down-cast eyes. "From the high-born of the Empire to those born at the mouth caves— every man knows the dangers of looking upon the Daughter of the Moon."

"So you have listened well to your people..."

"I listen for danger, my lady."

"Even now, in the presence of a queen who would rapture you, you bring your fears to my feet.

"I only seek to end the war."

She looked down on the encroaching death in his face- "And yet, you have created a battlefield."

Yama's eyes rolled back; taking in more pain.

The Daughter pulled a needle from her hair— she pulled a long strand of thin web, enough to fill the grip of her white fingers, and held them in her hand- "In case you should discover help," she said, giving the two items to Yama.

He saw the perfect white fingers lay the items at his side. Her wrists pivoting delicate suggestions of lust, each movement filled his attention, his temptation. Yama could not contain his eyes— they widened and followed the arm of the goddess upward, over the silver hem of her gown, across the brushstroke of her shoulder, falling into the wrinkle of a smile in her eyes. And there, inside her gaze, Yama glimpsed that primal perfection, an essence of beauty. Forever imbedded inside him, she made her rein inside him, a longing that is never sated.

And then she vanished— the sudden departure left Yama pining, his heart left exposed as the wilds around him cooed and laughed in the sudden reappearance of the darkness. The walls of night were abrupt, the trees creaking amongst one another, speaking in their aching language, syllables of ancient time.

Yama lied down to meet his death. As he lay, the moonlight which he received from the Moths were in the grass beside him. So with one grab he picked them up and threw them into the opening of the trees. The pieces of silver moon hung squirming in the sky, lighting the way around the treetops, its light seeping low into the trunks of the trees... Yama looked up and knew this would be his death— within a silent and silver forest tomb...

Yama wasn't aware how long he was asleep, but when he woke, he heard a wagon approaching on the road and a distant whistling song.

The whistling drew nearer with the romp of lanterns swinging and the old, aching progress of a wagon coming down the greenway. A moment later the wheels came to a stop outside his camp.

"The moonlight lead us to a corpse!" said a voice with the mummbling of pursed lips, holding a pipe.

Yama moaned.

The man hopped off his wagon and stood beside his mule- "He lives yet!" As the Traveler got a look at the man lying beside a dwindling fire, he noticed the cooking pot, the big spoon resting over it, the bowl still sitting on a stone in the hearth. "The son-of-a-bitch couldn't even finish his dinner."

The mule turned a square head into the man's shoulder, ears flipping, a handful of mosquitos dancing around his long eye-lashes.

"Hell's fire, Reggie, how do I help a fool like that?" he gestured to Yama lying with his arms holding his chest. "Damned drug fiend, likely."

The mule's eyes lowered with dumb attention at the roadside, tail flipping over his backside.

"Dammit, Reggie, you know how I feel about

kindness!"

The mule was turning his ears, listening to the wilderness.

"Reggie, dam you, old fool." The Traveler looked over at Yama and approached him. At closer examination, he noticed the firm fit of his clothing, the fine stitching, the brightness of the dye in the fibers. "Either he's an Empire fella', to some degree, or, he killed a man who was…" Then his eyes filled with a scheme: *kindness may pay-off yet,* he thought.

"Say!" the traveler walked his boots right next to Yama; stood there looking over him. "Hey, fella… I've got the cure for you."

Yama had been listening all along but couldn't bring himself to respond. Now he knew he had to address the man's interest. He opened his eyes and he saw his rough-made boots, scarred raw-hide with leather laces. His clothing was a patchwork of red, clayish brown, like bricks in a wall of a loose-fitting trench coat. His hat was wide, a dark saucer above slippery, jealous pits where his eyes were calculating, checking his schemes as they dealt the cards of a dying man.

"I don't much agree in helping people," his hands rested firmly inside his coat-pockets. "But I am not against doing favors for fellow road-tramps, like us."

Yama rolled over, the pain spitting through his

face, stomach burning, eyes heavy and red.

The man pulled a jar from inside his coat containing a technicolored glitter inside the glass. "Eat this butterfly," said the road-tramp. "If you do, it will cure your suffering…"

The pause from the traveler gave Yama time to feel his own desperation.

"In return, my friend, I'll take that bow, and the arrows too." His eyes gestured to Yama's weapon lying against a stump wrapped in English ivy. "Deal?"

Yama stirred. The weight of the offer made his aching intensify. The Bow of a Federation Archer was more than a tool… it was a companionship. Their initiation was to create the bow. To fell the Osage Orange. Carve it. Making multiple bows until the wood spoke to them. It was their training. The way to develop listening in their hands. A practice to achieve oneness. A martial companion who would stand as the only chance between the warrior and death.

Yama looked on the bow, slender in the firelight, the silver glitter of the string, unengaged and coiled around the weapon: *it has saved my life in so many instances… how do I honor the lives it has won, and lost, by dying today?*

His thought was suddenly disrupted— the Traveler suddenly turned a grim face toward a light approaching from the road. A tall covered wagon eased out of the darkness, the twinkle of lanterns highlighting the bulky frame of the machine.

"Hell's fire." The Traveler turned back to his wagon, drawing a sleek holster from a trunk at the bench. He slipped the short-sword from the leather, a sudden, grey flash in his dark hands, and then snapped it closed again, fitting it to his waste below his coat.

The covered wagon eased out of the darkness and came to a lumbering stop ahead of the other wagon. The pair of mares pulling the machine came to rest, grateful for the stop. There was no driver. A single light twinkled inside a small window in the carriage. A bolt unlocked with a *clunk*. A crack of light broke in the door. It swung open to a warm light, green curtains, the wafting of essential oils and mirr rolling out of the oversaturated air of the cabin. A thin figure dropped down, piercing green eyes inside a silver mane, a neck buried inside a scarlet scarf, a robe swishing the steps as she stepped down from the carriage door.

"You intrude on a man's grave, Tramp?" The old woman moved through the campsite and stopped at the hearth of the fire, her eyes criticizing the Traveler. "What have you done?"

"Who you calling a tramp, gypsy witch?" The Traveler tightened his stance- "He's poisoned.. not my doing..." His hand lingered at his belt.

"He's spiritually sick..." the woman was still and gazing on Yama with green-eye medallions inside blood-shot whites, dazzling with the peak of a drug-altered state. "You protect your pride with a long-knife beneath your coat..." the old woman looked down on Yama as she spoke to the Traveler. "Lend it to me... I will save this man."

The man bellowed with laughter- "Forget it, witch! You're strapped with that knife-blade around your thigh... no need for anything from me. Slit the man's throat with your own hand: own your own sins."

"Very well," the woman said with a smirk. *Doesn't hurt to keep a clean blade, if I can help it...* and she pulled a thin knife from below her robe.

"Hey, wait just a minute!" The Traveler stepped forward a step. The woman's eyes widened and fell over him like a shroud. He stopped with his hand buried under his coat, fingers on the hilt of his blade. "What devilry are you playing here, witch-woman?"

"Do you fancy some item this man carries?" the Woman gazed through his mind. "You cannot bring yourself to steal from a dying man. What's the wager you've made with this poor man?" She gestured to Yama, who was nearly out of his mind with fever.

The Traveler paused. An owl cooed from the deep night. Crickets were orchestral in the motionless forest. His eyes glanced at Yama's bow.

"Ahh…" The old Woman's dry lips turned upward with a snakish grin. "I expected you to reach deeper into his pockets than that…"

The Traveler's eyes slanted with suspicion- "He's worth more to me dead."

"I will preserve this man's life… do not interfere with my process."

Suddenly the Traveler's coat opened with a silver flash jutting out of his hand- the tip of the short-sword pressed into the Gypsie's robe, the man's hand clutching her neck: "He's worth more to me dead."

The Woman's eyes slid down to look closer at Yama. She had already seen everything about it him.. yet, she expressed surprise and gasped aloud.

"What is it?" The Traveler barked.

"This man is a Federation Warrior."

His eyes darted back and forth. "So what?"

He is a stupid tramp, she thought. *That will make this easier.* "Nevermind," she said to him.

"Tell me, witch!" The knife-blade pricked deeper between her ribs.

"Federal Warriors don't travel this far out of the Empire without company."

"Are you saying this is a trap?"

This tramp needs me to spell it out to him... "I don't suspect an ambush... they would have done it already..." The Woman's eyes looked up into the canopy, the moonlight that attracted her to this situation was still glimmering above the darkness. "He likely got this far on his own."

The Traveler was puzzling over the witch's words. She waited for his cumbersome mind to come up with the conclusion on his own.

Yama was only vaguely aware of what was happening. He was aware of a woman and man. He was aware that they were both interested in him, in some way... but as his reason faded with the pain, his intuition became clearer, his only remaining source of interface with the environment outside the darkness of his sickness. This subtle vibration sensed danger, shadows hung over the strangers, two devils bickering for his life...

He's still thinking about it?! The Gypsie didn't betray even the slightest impatience. She was pristine with waiting... "He must have had some good reason to run so far..." she lead the Traveler with a hint.

Suddenly she felt the tension in the sword draw back. *He's got it!*

"He's a deserter!" The witch felt the tremble of lust in the Traveler's knife.

"Ahh!" the old woman croaked. "That makes good sense, yes, yes…"

His eyes darted with possibility. "The reward would be…" and he caught himself, looked warily over the woman's shoulder and tightened his blade into the Gypsie's side. "Can you keep him alive long enough to get him back to the Empire?"

"I am certain of it…"

"What do you want out of this?"

The old woman's eyes quickened, a sharpened alertness intensified by the drug induced awareness, she licked her dry, peeling lips, a sticky saliva gathered at the corners of her mouth- "A witch desires possessions of an unworldy kind… the money is yours, tramp. Take it all."

The Traveler's eyes brightened. The knife fell away from the witches robe- "Do it," he said.

The witch returned to her carriage and came out again with a pouch; a single snake-skin folded back from the head, in one piece, so the empty skin made a water-tight pouch. She also brought a cedar box and a lamp and knelt at Yama's side, laying the pieces on the ground beside her.

Her hand waved over his face. Her lips murmured unrecognizable syllables. She turned the wick higher inside the lantern. A soft glow poured over the glistening beads of sweat on Yama's face. She lifted the glass cylinder of the lantern, holding a lump of resin in the flame until a pungent, spicy aroma wafted the campsite. She passed the smoke below Yama's nose, the aroma instantly bringing him back from a near state of delirium. He mumbled, his words belligerent.

The witch took her knife and cut a thin wound in his neck. She was quick to catch the fresh blood in a waxy leaf cupped into her bony, grey fingers. She took the red beads of blood and let them fall into the liquid contained by the snake skin. With her other hand she held a closed fist above Yama's chest, a small crystal dropping and swinging from a string looped over her finger. The pendulum swung along his vertical energy whilst her opposite hand shook the contents of the snake-skin.

The witch looked down on Yama with a grim face- "we need more life-blood," she hissed. She looked up at the Traveler, the whites of her eyes turned to a solid film, a deep silver, without pupil or iris. However, there was no doubt, inside those silver wells was a deep-seeing vision, peering through and through the wary Traveler.

"The soldier's got blood plenty for your devilry." His hand was firm on his knife.

"The spell is not going to revive him without another life-blood... it will only take a few drops."

"Use your own blood."

"I am already divined… we can use your blood… or…" she looked at the donkey standing bridled to the Traveler's wagon, its long ears turning toward the witches wilding energy.

The Traveler looked back at the animal- "Reggie?" he said under his own breath… Then he turned back to the witch in reserve- "Take it," and he held out his own arm.

In a flash the witch cut a thin, painless line into his forearm. Blood flowed swiftly. She gripped his wrist and turned the wound over, letting the blood run down to the hand, with the snake-skin she caught a single drop falling from the wrist. The Traveler could not feel the subtle energetic bond it created. But at that moment, in the grip of the witches icy hand, the snake-pouch in her opposite hand came alive! Its scales prickled to a sheen in the lamp-light, the headless flesh coiling upward around the arm of the old witch.

The Traveler tried to pull his arm away in a panic. For an instant, the witch resisted, a wicked grin in the corners of her eyes, she held his wrist inside her claw, silver eyes, deep and provoking. The man betrayed his terror, his heart leaping in sharp palpitations of fear, sweat trembling across his face in the sudden flare of the lantern-light. Her eyes enveloped his mind. In passing, as swift as a dream on a hot night, the witches silver glare pervaded him, eloped his senses, instantly, completely…

When the gypsy released his arm, she returned to her work with Yama as if nothing had happened. Even the Traveler couldn't confirm what had just happened. He looked at his arm. The cut had already turned to a scar. He looked at the old woman with anxious reverence as she held the pendulum over the soldier's chest.

"He is ready," she croaked, lifting the snake in both her hands. A palpable sense of divination pointed on this moment, the old-woman's wild mane of silver hair lifting, full and vibrant, her skin smooth, youthfulness in her face, her voice enchanted with an echo out of the dark hallows of the forest itself. Then she clenched Yama's bottom jaw, opening his mouth, she poured the contents of a dark, nearly onyx liquid into his throat. He tried to choke it back up, but she lifted his shoulders off the ground and lifted his chin to ease the potion down.

Yama was barely present. He could not grasp the happenings between the Witch and the Traveler, the contents of the ritual or even the taste of the dark liquid in his mouth... but Yama became, quite suddenly once the ritual began, sharply, and profoundly aware of himself. His attention was called back from a place where no effort stirred inside him. He was disassociated from the world, however, his sense of awareness was stimulated.

He experienced, now, after succumbing to death, a voice. A voice that beckoned as warmly as his mother. The same voice sounded also like a lover calling him to bed. A sister, calling him to play. A companion from deep within the catacombs of his longings. She was saying his name...

Yama... Come to me, Yama...

The Daughter of the Moon was there. He felt her presence. Remembering her eyes burning deep inside his heart. He was reaching out to her. Pouring himself at her feet. "Have you come to take me with you?"

She smiled, His hand reached to touch her robe.

Suddenly there was a seering pain in his body. An immediate rush back into the heat of his own skin, the clamping darkness of the night, a scream of pain leaping off his mouth. The potion of the witch-woman had become tongues of fire within Yama, decaying his body— his skin opening with fresh wounds...

The Traveler, seeing Yama's body falling apart, stepped forward- "Hey, witch! You said you would keep him alive—

The witchwoman's hand snapped and her eyes pierced him- "Do not interfere!"

The man was already stepping away before she finished her command. He was startled by how immediately he obeyed— fear struck him when he realized, her voice had compelled him to move, a spell over his muscles. But the truth was greater than that. She had trapped his lifeblood into the ritual. He, along with Yama, were bewitched into her will.

Yama... the Daughter of the Moom was still calling him. Yama wanted to be with her. A place in him longed to be enveloped in every suggestion inside this woman's voice. To linger in that place inside the voice of a woman. Though all men may not follow the call into bewilderment and war... many deny their bodies of her truth... even more deny their hearts.

The woman behind the voice drew closer inside Yama's mind. The night was breaking with subtle ribbons of dawn. A soft moisture fell out of the trees and touched his feverish cheeks.

"I am here to help you." She said, a warmth surrounding her words.

Yama opened his eyes and saw the face of the Daughter of the Moon, her milky hands touching his burning forehead, and her deep, rich hair falling over her neck. The Daughter's eyes flowed through him. His heart pouring with sentiment. His mind, bent on her perfection. His lips murmured, "my beloved," yet, the Witch silenced him.

"Who the hell are you?" the Traveler slipped his knife toward a female stranger standing at the edge of the camp, her back loaded with a pack, a top-knot of bronze hair gathered at the crown of her head, and a bow fitted with an arrow in her hands.

The Traveler showed his knife to her- "You've lost your way... Move along—now."

The woman had come out of the forest, following the low orbs of moonlight through the forest canopy. She stood silently observing. Her eyes were strong, missing nothing, with the deep glimmer of a bright doe. The poise in her hands showed her caution. Her body was pivoted with a careful steadiness. The Traveler's warning did not sway her.

"Move along..." he repeated, the knife-blade glinting for her to see.

"What's your business with this dying man?" The woman's words were direct and without emotion, her eyes looking down at the witch-woman, who was concealing her face, bent over Yama's broken body.

"Our business is none of yours—"

"The moonlight has lead us all to the same place..." Her eyes motioned toward Yama- "Is this the man who set the orbs above this campsite?"

The witchwoman stirred, a slight gesture of annoyance, not unnoticed to the stranger's keen eye.

"What state did you find this man?" she persisted.

"Fuck off, bitch, or I'll stick you and throw your body into a wet ditch for the animals."

"What is this man's name?" she persisted.

The Traveler took a step leading with the knife. The stranger brew back her bow. It ached with tension. The tip of the arrow shining against the smooth arch of Osage Orange.

The Traveler took another step back.

The witchwoman spat and parted a gap in her wild, silver mane. She looked up at the Traveler and with a flash of her hand, commanded him to strike. Against his own will, he found himself leaping across the campsite, diving with his long-knife toward the stranger.

There was a sudden snap and a flash of something dark moving through the campsite. The traveler dropped to his knees and toppled backward with an arrow standing out of his neck. There was no hesitation before the witch-woman was crawling over Yama's body, down on all-fours, her silver mane bristling like the back of a hyena. She sprang onto the stranger, the shuffling of struggle, the witch-woman screaming and the stranger's hand lunging a knife firmly through her ribs.

A long, exasperated gasp exited the old woman's body. A sinister expression passed through her face, a delighted evil that gathered into the corners of her eyes and mouth, producing a kind of porcelain smile void of all warmth. The spell had been broken. The body of the old woman rolled to the stranger's feet and did not get back up. Stillness fell over the camp.

Now the woman urgently moved toward Yama. She came closer, kneeling beside him- "My name is Kathrana."

Yama made no response.

Kathrana unexpectedly found a needle and thread lying on the ground beside him. She shouldered her pack to the ground and unbound the cordage of a side-pocket. After gathering the broken body of the soldier, she took the needle and thread, and moving like familiar waters, threaded the web through the head of the needle. Then she took cloths from her pack and the pickings of a long, fleshy leaf. She ripped a bite and chewed the meat of the leaf, filling her cheeks and gradually spitting its juices into Yama's wounds. Meanwhile, she sang a prayer behind a full mouth of poultice.

Yama's body trembled with the purging of the venom. From a distant place, he thought he was hearing a song sung by the Daughter of the Moon: "she has come back for me," he thought. Enamored, lost deep inside the fantasy of her shoulders diving like porpoise through his mind, he remained with his eyes closed, absorbed inside his thoughts of Her.

But the song he heard was Kathrana's, a chant of her native village— a place long behind her.

Reluctantly, Yama began to stir from his dream.

His first words stumbled from his tongue- "Are you the Daughter of the Moon?"

With a leaf hanging against her chin, Kathrana pricked Yama in the arm with the tip of the needle:

He recoiled his hand and opened his eyes wide: "Ahhya!"

"Good, you have feeling in your nerves again..." she said, taking a cloth and wiping the drool from her neck, which was the aloe that saved his blood. "Don't waste your energy on silly questions. You should rest. Drink this."

She helped Yama drink from a small water bladder, then laid back down, a soothing sweetness flowing through him from the liquid. He listened to her advice and closed his eyes, falling into a dreamless sleep.

When his eyes opened again, the first thing he saw was Kathrana, sitting against the roots of a tree. He remembered her eyes were busy, matter-of-factly. She was focused on sowing her pack with the left-over string she used to close his wounds. There was sun on her face and a pleased smile on her lips.

"Good, you're awake. Sit up if you can. Drink water."

"I was dreaming about you..." said Yama, his eyes glittering like the silver lining of a moon. "You enchanted me."

"Bah!" Kathrana was sharp with a flick of her hand. "Your were dreaming about some daughter of a moon." Kathrana did not look up from the task in her hands. "I am Kathrana, daughter of—" she cut her words off, let her bag drop into her lap, and she looked at him in a long pause- "I am a long way from who I used to be," she said with some tension. Her eyes stayed with him: "Tell me your name."

"Yama, son of Dapha, warrior of the Federation, seitch of the Koda." His words were recited.

"You speak like a dead man."

Yama was shocked: "this comes from the one I owe my life?"

"You speak like a soldier... but I saw a soldier die here today." She bit the string off the needle and put the leftovers in a small pouch. "I've been wanting to patch that hole for miles now," she said. With admiration for her work, she stood and laid the bag at her feet.

Yama gazed at his own hands- "I can't go back." Yama held his breath.

"Neither can I," said Kathrana.

"What am I, if not a soldier?"

"Whatever you want to be."

Yama shrugged- "In my birth village I was a poet."

"So be it... Yama, the wandering poet."

He nudged his chin northward- "Where does this road lead?"

"Someplace different..." Kathrana pulled a buckle at her waste, closing a cloak into her belt, water glugging from satchels she carried at her sides, a knife at her hip. "I'm going North."

"Let's go together..."

Kathrana swung her saddlebag onto her back, a quiver of long-arrows clattering, and she paused, standing over him... "Will you carry your weight of the pack?"

"Yea...of course..." and he smiled, looking up at her- "Hey! You still have a piece of leaf on your chin."

She giggled, wiping her lips, and then frowned with a playful cock in her head- "Look at'ya, lying around with a road ahead of us— when are you ready to get going?"

1.

<u>Initiation</u>

*You may never fulfill all the needs
of those you love.
However, you can
fulfill all that is required
to love yourself.*

Wildling

Take me with you.

Unfold with me, set free into this savage night.

Lay me down below a peyote twilight.

Take me with you into the running horses

and run with me, wild darling.

Like grasslands and wildfires

turn me in our sleepless bed.

Lets be brave

unfold the fear in our hearts

to discover a new creature, innate

and infinitely more intelligent

than we've ever known ourselves

to Be.

Take me. Come with me.

Keeping your Sword Sharp

Where do I follow you, beloved?

How far are you intending to drive me

away from the comforts of my village?

You keep the fire of my heart—

I am the empty lantern

desire is the wicking of oil inside me.

Warriors cross this road, from time to time,

and I ask them about their journey.

I ask them about the animals in the wild

and the lovers of the towns:

"Tell me, traveler,

how do you become lost in love for a night

and then continue the path after morning?"

There is a light in their eyes

of laughter.

That laughter can also become a sword.

Their hearts open gentle doors

yet they stride in the bewilderment

of dangerous territory.

They open their hands

weathered by the years of practice

and they say to me:

"Little brother, you're a dead-man, anyway

so make your Love bold

and sweeping—

but for God's sake, never forget

your sword's

gotta' stay sharp."

Hero's Journey

In these easy

whispering hills

All sleep warmly

in timber dens, all

think soundly

in peaceful beds—

Through a narrow door in our hearts

Heroes are combed out of the grasses.

Devastation flushes them down

from worn and weakening nests

by need, by fate

as one by one

fear swells beneath their wings

we learn to fly

across thresholds

of wild frontiers.

2.

There are balances that the Universe

Doesn't show us.

Mysteries to how it works

We may never define.

The cosmos doesn't shine the light on all things—

Sometimes, we must see by way of the shadow, sometimes

The absence of light tells our secrets.

Secrets within Secrets

Yama looked high above their camp, set in the wild grasslands, agape at the view before him, raptured in the infinitude of stars beyond stars in the visible night. Something in his eyes reminded Kathrana of the hazel gaze of the Gwen Eden, shaman of her childhood village, sitting outside the giant-horse-hide shelter.

"This is Kenya—" the Gwen Eden waved her hand across the night-sky above her birth lands, the great belt of dust inoculated with the glistening bulbs of white stars, blue giants, warm red dwarfs, and the twinkling of their brightest siblings burning in open darkness toward the horizons. "This is mystery within mystery within mystery... Shanganga, god of the eastern Sun, rides upon his wild stallion, through the Kenya wilding, leading the undying herds. We look to them, we follow their burning dust, we perform ritual in their honor, and in return, they have given us their power, the backs of the Saraf Horses, a connection to the mightiest of the Dengu herds." ...

Kathrana put her hand on Yama's arm and gestured toward the view above them: "In my village-tongue we called this, *Kenya*," and her hand swept across the sky in warm demonstration.

Yama observed the dust-plains of starlight ahead of her gesture- "I was born in an urban section of the Enyana Empire," he said.

"The City of Light?" The tone in her voice betraying wonder.

Yama nodded- "I looked out the window from my bed-mat at the House of Qi Khan Namo, The Shining Palace. We lived in a quarter of the city close to the royal manors. My father was a wealthy businessman who sold textiles. I joined the military to avoid becoming my father's apprentice in the business. So I became an archer in the seitch Koda instead... in the city, there are always lights burning, strong and white. They shine bright throughout the night. The Empire proudly pushes away the darkness. They did not see how it threw away the stars, too."

"No stars?"

"No stars..."

Suddenly a single light crystalized above them and flung itself across the sky in a stream of white dust. Yama's hand nearly leapt out of Kathrana's gentle touch as he pointed up at the bright light: "what was that?!"

She couldn't help but laugh at his innocent wonder... it was something she loved about him- "My village calls it, *Amori...* The white torch carried by the consort of Shanganga."

Yama focused on the blinking of a bulbous star suspended deep within the belt of backlit dust- "I never imagined the sky had such secrets."

"My people say that Amori joined Shanganga on his journey through the cosmos so he might have light through the darkness between the stars."

"Do you still believe the stories of your home-people?" Yama looked at her, the features of her face silhouetted by the simmering light of the fire.

Yama noticed Kathrana retreat from his question, her hands turning to soft fists— "I've left my village for many reasons."

Yama sat in silence, returning his sight to the sky- "The constellation Jengu," he pointed to the bright and sharply focused stars in the low southern sky. "It was a familiar one often seen by farmers from their country houses. They use to tell me he was a warrior, an Archer of the predawn Empire, high in the North beyond the Feurengul. He once killed five hundred men from a clifftop before the soldiers could scale the ridge. I use to imagine what it was like to stand like a hero on that mountainside. I use to climb into towers and play the whole scene. Once I fell from the second story of a rooftop and broke my right arm. I think it was the gods trying to tell me something…"

Kathrana's brow bent with intrigue- "What were they telling you?"

"My right arm is my shooting arm. It took me a long time to strengthen that arm for a bow. Longer than the other archers of the seitch. It formed a relationship with this arm… I remember the pain of that experience every time I draw to shoot. I remember the story of Jengu… and when I remember the boy who once dreamed of becoming an Archer, I am reminded of all the men slain under the banner of that dream…"

Kathrana studied the dark lines in her lover's face. Memory of the sage-woman was still burning fresh in her mind; the whiteless gaze of dark hazel eyes, staring at her from the reed mat, shaking a pouch of gems in the brown, gentle tremble of her hands.

"I will not take husband, Gwen Eden." Kathrana told the sage decidedly. "I will not take husband. I will not make the next knot of our ancestral braid... I will not accept the love of Depoah Manu."

The sage-woman let the gemstones fall inside a wide basket. She studied them with careful consideration. After many moments, her voice finally spoke with a conserved compassion: "You will leave the lands of your birth, Kathrana. You will separate yourself from your people— you will not be initiated according to our tribe's tradition. If you wish to live in the world, then, you must be initiated by the world..."

Her deep, impassive stare closed behind the wrinkling of eyelids. The chortle of frogs sang in the night, a gentle wind rippling at the doorway, fire dancing at the center of the shelter- "I instruct you to stay here until you have matured from the years of the suckling calf. Stay until you are at the age of Chenu, a woman, and then you may leave to find love in the wilding world."

Kathrana tightened her posture, lifting her chin, she closed her hands into fists-"My mind will not be changed by waiting."

The Gwen Eden's hazel gaze drew a deep concentration over Kathrana- "You do not have to trust the love of others, my child…" Wood from the fire sang from the hearth, fire dashing higher. "However, you must make stride to repair your relationship to your own heart. Depoah Manu is the love that sheds the false for a deeper reality. Depoah Manu will find you… If you resist, your resentment will continue creating a war against the flesh of your spirit."

Kathrana remembered this moment with clarity. Holding Yama's hand, dawn began unfolding in the east… She still did not fully understand the sage-woman, however, she held the memory with her like a secret message.

Then she turned to Yama who was still gazing up at the night-sky- "what has become of your boy-hood dream, Yama?"

He sat quietly for several moments before speaking… "It was only a dream."

She continued looking at him as his eyes slowly fell away toward the opening eastern sky. A caring feeling swept over Kathrana, her hand still holding his…

"When I was in my homeland," said Yama. "I thought there was nothing of mention beyond the sky I knew. Then I joined the military and I never looked beyond the blood in the dirt. And here I am with you now, discovering a much greater reality was always above my head, a greater truth, merely awaiting our eyes to see it."

Yes— thought Kathrana, holding her eyes on the frame of Yama's dark face in the breaking light... *perhaps the mystery will show itself... if we care to look.*

Wild Hearts

Burning as bright as ice

the night sky shines.

A cloud splashing against space

is cut to pieces

in light's disrobing manners.

The seeds we shared last night

are aching

for a season of good work.

I've quit my job

tallying the payoff

year after year of our loving—

Let the neighbors see us

standing below the belly of a star

under wind and light

splitting every seed inside

our wild

messy hearts!

Untitled

I see worlds spinning around fools.

I have known myself to sing

the praises of broken cups.

I can no longer accept

an image, a dollar

for life's true majesty.

The breaking of the night

reveals the wars that were gathered

while I slept.

Their voices cry out about republics

and love.

But I cannot fight these battles.

There must be Reality found within.

The center of Being

a hidden gravity

bending truth between our breasts.

Nature

No lip can speak truth forever.

But a gentle eye can see itself

and actions are a revolution.

Share the working hands of your truth.

The truth must come from somewhere—

We have been given a key. Find the door.

Challenge Truth to make it grow.

We divide ourselves amongst other people

and put our faith into ancient stones

expecting them to govern our aggressions.

Not so. Violence

is the radical climate of our own self creation.

Uproot a nation in your life

and free yourself—

a wild opening awaits.

Stand beside rivers too huge

to pass.

Bend your values

into the arches of your bridge.

Practice them

until the water bows to your Art.

Show Nature

you know

you exist.

Show Nature you know

you exist.

Many Names of Love

These times when we are hungry

for the core of ourselves

are also when we muster our courage

to start knocking down walls

of our own house—

we open the kitchen into the garden

pull our tables and chairs into the lawn

and see our neighbors for the first time…

How do we begin, from here

to discuss the frightened tenderness's

that have kept us staying the same?

We try to keep our heads cool

feeling what we feel

without calling it something it is not—

meanwhile the *need* in the world

stokes our flames…

Perhaps one day we will share with each other

the depth of reasons why

both in fire

and in bed

we have been calling out

the many names

of Love?

Winter Grass

Here I find myself again

in this House

where simple tongues

say simple things

yet always prefer the quiet

spicy lips

of tulsi and bourbon tea.

Just when I had decided

to make this green settlement

another home

I discover again

the sleeping winter grasslands

inside my soul.

This poem isn't about me

or you—

the spring storm inside

my bedroom window

throws me over this page

the way my desire sometimes slides

like rain over you.

You are the same

This Poetry

and Love— I

am only a field

of hard winter wheat;

You invited a passage

an earnest migration

I couldn't resist.

Now I've become the harvest
the sickle of working moons
gradual handfuls of winnow
blowing against the corner steps
of your Garden.

Candlestick

Here we are

        I sit to listen to this candlelight

perhaps to see a King of another

world orbit, moving over

a flame so gentle as my own.

I am no Emperor— only a poet

who can afford his own candlesticks.

        Beside a cup of tea

I comb these words

from the mess of my unwashed

never-shorn heart—

        My ambition to attain

praise

hardens between us

like the wax which runs

too far from the light.

And though my mouth is a bucket

of stones—

my tongue is still softening

in daily centimeters of fire

traveling a wick which runs

straight through the Heart of me.

Wild Baskets

Go into the wild forests of your truth.

Let yourself be afraid.

Learning to stand with fear in your heart

is like learning to stand with a bear—

if you stand true

Nature will see who you Are.

This is courage.

We pour ourselves out into thought

wasting the hands of our maker.

Live from the Earth.

Till, sow, and grow.

Love, work, and celebrate.

Simple truth never dies.

Our defensive worlds may divide our loving.

Unruly humanness may pull us apart.

But I will love you

with knives against my breast

I will dance— and you

will do to my heart

what the weaver has done

with her baskets.

Untitled

As fear shakes me at the ankles

Love drags me from the shirt.

I argue with Love.

I try to convince it that I am

already defined... *Leave me as I am!*

It doesn't say a word about it.

Love just comes into my house

pulling on the flesh of my heart

as she puts the knife in my hand.

The instrument of my body

cries out from the song in her touch.

The pen within my eyes

takes note of a truth.

Don't seek my words— my lips

are still within you.

Don't remember my face—

the memory inside the body

becomes a bed for our longing.

Lift my legs and play music with me.

Spread open your tongue

and fill my broken ear

with a vibration of your truth.

Fiercely Hot Karma

When we found each other, we were lovers— swimming

below an erotic lantern.

After long afternoons below

the white gables of thought.

After our days of breaking rocks

to collect the salt inside them—

We come, at last, to lay

our sexual trembling

into each other's arms.

Hands touching hands

lips pressed to ears

fingers to mouth

feet to shoulders

skin washed in heat

hair flashing

across the bend in your neck

Galloping towards the white waters

of our coming

we take a breath

we dive

we peak

tremble at the plinth

and then we fall back on pillows

with our lips ready for any word

of truth

like slices of apples

and pears.

We close our thighs

like a book falls shut

after finishing the last line

of a poem.

We emerge from the bedroom

with our hair ruffled

and a rough power of loving

splinted our hearts

willow baskets for a truth.

We will lose ourselves again, my dear,

we were never together

forever.

Thirst always empties our jars

returning us again

and again— doorstep

to doorstep

seeking the waters of our desires

that we might satiate the dry seeds of our bodies

wash ourselves together with beautiful people

tipping our bodies over the bed

for new tastes

new meanings, and even

new thorns of medicine

which we will grow together

entangled

and involved

in Love.

3.

Build a fire of remembering
every night
to do the work that bends light
into a permanent season of beauty.
Enter that wilderness of yourself
braving the animals
with shoulders standing
nearly taller than your courage.

Bison Chase

When the stalkers reached the alcove in the terrain below them, Yama took a deep breath. *Today is the killing*, he thought.

The firewall was lit in the grass, burning in a long line of dark smoke through the prairieland, flames creeping higher. A hundred yards away, the faces of paleo-bison were lifting their woolen faces from the grass, chewing, meandering.

Ten thousand strong, Yama had guessed. *They are smelling the fire. The trigger is stirring inside them*. Yama shook his head.

Kathrana approached riding a white mare to his side. "You're tense."

Yama didn't reply, which made his tension grow deeper.

"Stay in form this time," she continued. "Lets just do what we came to do."

The stalkers crouched low in the alcove, wrapping their arms inside the greyish wolf-skins around their shoulders. With their spears and atlatls leaning against the turf, their faces turned toward Yama and Kathrana on the hillside, waiting.

A low ceiling of grey, witchy clouds began to set low and drizzle. The mist was reaching up from the trees in wet curtains. Yama's eyes were flinching under the tension in his jaws. This was the way he felt before every battle. Every man in the federacy of the Emperor's army faced immutable fear before a battle. Every man would visit the lips of their holiest demi-spirit, or remembering the love of a wife, the best of them summoning their courage... Yama would feel this gathering tension before every battle— and recently, he had been feeling it again, before a bison chase.

Yama's eyes looked beyond the alcove into a great expanse of savannah, occupied by the meandering bodies of the bison. Smoke from the firewall was blowing toward them from a southerly push. The weather was changing. The bison were lying down... old farmers from the countryside use to say the rain would come when the cattle were lying down. He always believed it.

"Here they come," said Kathrana with a sudden reserve. Yama heard the hooves of several more riders approaching through the soft, snowy ground. The first of the smugglers to the hilltop was Dakkard Johnson, an alpha character amongst the paleo game hunters. He brought the rarest skins from out of the wild. His shipments were consistent, and "consistency makes me too goddamn valuable to have killed." And this kept his pocket full.

He pulled his bay mare just ahead of Kathrana and looked down into the valley with a grin that curled like the ends of smoke. "Never a day that the smell of a fire doesn't remind me of profit." The slight tremble in Dakkard's deep eyebrows betrayed his delight. His eyes observed the long line of fire below them, stroking his mustache- "Poor conditions for the firewall."

"It won't get too high," Kathrana noticed as the flames thinned out through the snow damp grass, excess smoke pouring itself into capes across the slopes. "That smoke will impair our visual of the stalkers."

"Where are the Hamerson boys?"

"With Handock's team," a fella was quick to answer from Dakkard's possie.

"They're right in front of us," said Yama, looking down at the grey cloaks crouching in the alcove. "They're watching for the signal."

"Well, you give it, then, Yama— this is your chase."

Kathrana glared at him. The other smugglers stirred in their saddles with a hint of disease.

Yama took another deep breath. Inside his chest was anxiety clamoring, setting fire to his chest, milling his thoughts into warnings.

"Are you going to call them?" Kathrana snapped with sudden impatience.

Dakkard was pulling a pouch from his jacket, rolling a cigarette. A heavy stillness hung on the air. A steady unfolding of white breath poured from the deep hoods of the party.

Yama's heart was beating heavier. To the west he gauged the distance of a long basin which dropped from a cloistering of foothills into a lower steppe of grasslands. He noticed the hills themselves were carved with banks of stone, long scars within the grey winter landscape. The basin was their "drop-ground". Kathrana was adamant about it: "The basin would be a sure place to coral the herd... it will get the job done- no fuss..."

"Yea, it's straightforward..." Yama said the day before as they planned the chase. "It looks a little too shallow... the fall might not kill them... I've got one of those feelings about it."

"Spare me..." Kathrana rolled their map and stuffed it into a saddle-bag. "Lets get this done."

They were on the terrain with the fortune of fresh snow... on the morning of the chase they saw a Dengu Tiger has passed through the area. "He's here for the Bison." said Dakkard.

Kathrana wrung her hands; her eyes sank into a pit of fear: "Maha Puchu," she said. "They were a terror for our cattle in the village... one of them took a boy..." She shivered with the memory, lowering her eyes.

"They are a fine prize," said Dakkard. "They sell for a rich price... we can mark the hazard pay to any amount we please. No one would question the danger."

Yama felt the edginess from the smugglers as they waited for him to call the Chase. The huddled grey-wolf pelts of the stalkers were restless, faces puzzled.

"Why are we waiting?" said Kathrana with a low voice, only for him.

Yama swallowed a lump of anger at her impatience... but he knew the time had come— he couldn't put it off. He took one last look northwest toward the basin, back to the wide expanse of the herd, and finally, the expecting hunters in the alcove.

He grabbed his hat, his hair messed into a top-knot at the crown of his head, and he whirled it three times above him before pulling it over his brow again.

The stalkers began to move right-away. From their place they spread out and pursued the open field just beyond. Yama saw the other two parties of stalkers, specks in the distance, scattering from hiding, their movement stamping dark lines through the grass as they encroached the herd.

"There they go," croaked Dakkard.

"Lets get in position." Kathrana steered away and galloped down the long slope into the lower fields. Dakkard followed her. The smugglers filed their horses behind with the slush of melting snow at their hooves.

There was a restless hush amongst the Bison as they approached the herd. *The trigger is moving*, thought

Yama, listening to the tension in the air. The first bison stood only an arrow's reach away, its shoulders towering out of the grass.

They all sat on horseback, side by side, the smoke of the fires low and black, drifting through their visual of the stalkers.

The air was heavy and gathering. Yama felt the ache of rain in his hands. An archer's hands: his fingers always knew when the weather would change.

We need the herd running southwest, Yama thought. His eyes looked beyond the backs of the bison at the southern expanse. A restless sky blew over a sea of grassland.

"This herd is settled down" said Dakkard, hanging on to the damp cigarette between his lips. "Not inclined to budge on our account."

"If we ride in close, it might get them started," Kathrana's eyes intent on the first line of cows.

Yama was trying to spot the stalkers through the smoke… There! He saw one— the grey coat of wolf standing out of the grass. A spear was levered over his shoulder. He was a throw away from the giant head of an old heifer jostling her horns side to side.

"They're about to set the trigger," said Yama aloud. *But it's too soon,* he thought to himself.

The smugglers readied their bows, tied scarves across their faces, settled their legs deeper into their saddles.

There was hesitance in the stalkers, Yama could feel it. There was great danger in this moment. Bison had stopped grazing, attention turned towards the wolves approaching. Bellows echoed out across whole expanse of the herd.

The stalkers continued to hesitate.

"They're going to lose the advantage." Kathrana said with anxiousness

"They must be waiting for a bigger firewall."

"Well they're not gonna' get it. Rains coming." Dakkard threw away his cig and buried his nose into a kerchief.

Yama opened his fingers wide, closed them again, sensing the onset of a shift.

"Let's ride in!" Kathrana jumped.

"Stay!" Yama was sharp. "The tension is building."

"Yea! Having one of those beasts trample a Hamerson boy will make things real fucking tense!" Her tone was accusing.

"Riding in too soon might run the herd straight through them!" Yama had a sense for this moment, better than any of the others— Dakkard knew this, so he waited, watching.

"Yama! What is with you?"

Suddenly Yama felt it... a new feeling arrived from the southeast, a conundrum of wind billowed through the pines of the northern hills, the firewall fanning higher above the fields. A bluster of the incoming rain filled the grasslands. The sudden approach of the storm brought a kind of confusion to the herd.

Yama lifted his bow high, his face filled with heat, he released a blood-running cry. The cry ignited his emotions into a rushing of vitality. His neck went red. His eyes were a terror. Kathrana knew him this way— she never crossed him when he was ready for the killing.

The stalkers heard the cry. They felt renewed by it. With the firewall whipping toward their backs they pounced from the grass in unison, yelping, howling, bows snapping in their arms. Arrows landed into the huge wall of ribs that made the first line of cows. They bucked in anger. One of the heifers sprinted. Turned. Faced the stalkers head-on.

Yama saw it happening. It was a crucial moment— *we want them running southwest.*

A folly of spears sent the heifer dropping, the huge arch of her back rolling over in the grass, its mighty horns teetering, lumping to the ground. At this moment the rest of the herd escalated. Their eyes staggered for escape. The first of them rumbled in flight.

Yama was already charging. Kathrana a pace behind him. He was howling with all the might of his belly, his lungs swollen with fire. The smugglers followed nearby, Dakkard fitting an arrow into his long-bow and loosing it at the staggering herd.

When the trigger was set, it was unmistakable; a cascading thunder of earth-driven panic. A unified reaction—these great animals set into motion created a tremendous and unyielding avalanche of fear.

Yama was leading the chase. Beside the tremendous roar of the herd he, carried by his mare Drogo, made an aggressive course along the running bison. Kathrana rode swiftly into Yama's wing, held there, a grace of wind over his shoulder. She rode in oneness with her mare, Elem, flowing over the terrain as swift as a rushing stream.

Yama rode in closer to the herd. He drew attention to a young bull. With his bow drawn the arrow released itself. The bull-calf stumbled, changed direction to run deeper into the herd. Yama reloaded and sprung an arrow to the next cow ahead. Kathrana followed with a second. The animal veered right, crossing them, grass clipping through her hooves, snow slinging off the back of her legs. Kathrana sent another arrow soaring into the swerving path of the cow. On the far side, Dakkard ran in close, sent an arrow piercing her at the fringe of the mien, through the heart.

The animal's legs skid to a stop. The weight of her body pivoted forward. Her mien shook and her horns danced. She landed with a graceful lunge of her breast into the grass. *The earth took her well*, Yama thought. Kathrana couldn't help but notice: *Died strong, she did*!

The landscape was climbing from the low meadow into a rising of knolls, offering a wide view of the far-reaching spread of the herd. Yama turned uphill and looked back for a visual— the herd was dovetailing across the terrain, dividing like mighty rivers branching apart across the steppes. From here he spotted an arm of the herd diverging toward the ridge, a grouping of about one hundred and fifty, leading a strong run toward the upper ridgeline. He looked back at Kathrana who was returning his gaze from downhill, and he knew in her eyes that she had already seen it! They reacted together, picked up full gallop into the herd again. The smugglers followed their lead, sparing their arrows and spreading open like tail feathers behind Yama and Kathrana, keeping the pressure on the herd.

They rode in close to the diverging arm, close enough to notice their plush winter coats pillowing over their shoulders, the white steam blowing from panting breaths. Yama and Kathrana had their attention on the same bison, both knowing which one to bring down... with arrows fitted, feathers at their cheeks, both felt the crack of their bows in unison. They hit their mark! The cow danced out of stride, staggered rightside. Kathrana was already set for another shot. A flash of her bow launching, followed by a thin, dark flash. In a fright the heifer tripped across her own feet, rolled around and in a tremendous dive to the ground, plowed through the stride of a fleeing comrade. There was immediacy in their blunder. A dramatic tumbling head over head, the back legs of the heifer dancing airborne over the other cow.

Yama and Kathrana did not stop, and as soon as the hefers fell, the arm of bison broke from the main herd. Yama drove to the inside— a handful of the bison did not follow group. Instead they fumbled back, trying to cross through the course of their chasers!

"Blind running was the most dangerous," Dakkard had warned them. "Leg for a leg in our line of business."

Suddenly the flank of a huge cow grazed through Kathrana's stride. Her mare dodged and dropped her front hooves to the grass, skid to a fullstop, turning Kathrana around on Elem's back and dropping her to the ground. Kathrana rode every chase bareback, with a blanket and reins, nothing more. She hit the earth and lay in the grass with her blanket twisted across her hips and her back flat in the grass, looking up at the heavy flow of storm clouds.

She lay for a moment, disoriented by the sudden break in dynamism, the impact buzzing through her body. The sound of hooves, the thunder of open running, filled her ears. The grass wrapped itself around her, a cold, damp bed.

Once she stood she saw Elem circling, flustered. They made eye contact and she came to a repose. Kathrana gave a shrill whistle and the mare responded with a whiney. They met each other and re-mounted,

Kathrana's eyes devouring the situation ahead of them, reorienting their place.

A smuggler had rode out of line and was approaching. "Are you hurt?"

"No I'm fine." Her words were brittle. *I'm still shaken*, she thought.

She made a quick glance behind them. The two heifers who were brought down to separate the herd lay in mounds of wool and muscle in the grass, arrows prickled through their miens. Ahead, Dakkard was taking a team high to beat the separated herd to the ridgeline, preventing them from spreading apart at the top. Smugglers carried the back, driving the line. Yama was taking the right: she noticed how headstrong he had become, separating himself from the others and running the bison with a challenging drive. *He hasn't even noticed I've fallen out of line,* a pang struck her.

The herd was driving west.

"We should catch up," said the smuggler, looking up the west bank of hills.

Kathrana swallowed her hurt and asserted her voice over Elem's shoulder- "Neoma pah eujeya!" she cried in her village tongue. The mare's silver eyes quickened and they galloped headlong in pursuit of the chase-line.

Kathrana picked up Yama's wing, the flicker of a glance over his shoulder indicated he was aware of her. Together they collected their momentum against the animals and veered the herd northwest while the rest of the team closed in from the southeast. The grouping that broke-off from the main herd was now cresting the top of the ridge.

If they are driven too hard they might scatter, Kathrana was thinking.

Lets not hurry to drive them, Yama commented to himself.

Kathrana glanced over at Yama— he looked back at her and knew they were thinking the same thing. He raised his bow arm high: the other smugglers saw the signal and maintained a tight lead on the left wing of the herd as they curved over the crown of the ridge. The slope panned into a high meadow below the S-curve ridge of a higher foothill. Foothills above foothills, the slopes gradually climbed into the cracked veins of dark stone jutting through the glacial blankets of the Puhgamu mountains.

Pines were standing out of a mist that had settled between the scattered woods. The head of their current course aimed further west where the landscape flattened and they could drive the bison across the plateau. From here, a balance had to be held until the basin line. Kathrana was gifted at sensing this particular rhythm of tension.

Yama rode out of center to let Kathrana take the lead: she was right behind him to pick it up. The herd opened a little. The smugglers loosened their pressure. They had about a mile to drive the bison now. The basin would be on the far side where the slopes of the western foothills suddenly dropped off into the greatness of the Dengu Plains, as far and wide as the southern horizon.

Yama was driving the right wing of the herd, closing in tight against their formation; he was known to dive in close, encroaching on a bison's stride. Kathrana disagreed with his technique, taking time to criticize.

"You are not thinking of others when you act this way."

"Aggression sharpens the fear of the herd." Yama would say to argue his way. "A lion at their shoulder gives them more to run for."

With a condescending sharpness in her delivery, she would reply: "Lions hunt in prides, my dear."

Kathrana couldn't deny, however, that Yama was the best for subverting the line. She observed him and saw the right wing was under his complete control. The other smugglers were a supportive back line. Dakkard and another rider held the western line. All together they moved, organically, at times letting the bison run with the lead but keeping their fear in-check; together they charged the basin in a steady rushing of hooves.

It was a moment of fluid Harmony, Yama noticed. No arrows were fired. There was a moment of mutual balance between fear and pursuit. An unbroken understanding of each player's position in the chase. Each player, neither forbearing or rash, maintained their presence, settled and steady on their course to the basin.

Yama noticed Kathrana, balanced over her mare's back, a red blanket between her thighs, mud whiplashed across the leather wrappings around her calves. Elem's strides were deep and her rider's commands were, to her, a breeze inside a sail. Kathrana's attention was in a trance of intelligence. She was at one with her comrade. She was bearing the oneness in the herd; hearing the paces of their collective motion. She also rode with a kind of empathy for the stakes of this mission— eager for the payoff, also holding a kind of courage within the directness of its dangers. "Beauty like a sword," Yama often said about Kathrana. And Yama thought: "I have knelt to pray at the edge of that blade— and god has returned with everything short of my neck."

Yama saw the basin line approaching. He had been watching it grow near and it seemed to suddenly encroach many paces ahead, leaping forward with a few unexpected bends in the landscape. It was nearing faster than he first had judged, so he threw his arm high, pulled out of form and backed down the line to take the lead from Kathrana. It was a surprise to her. So Kathrana picked up her gallop and made contact with Yama. Her eyes flashed over him. He replied with a direct stab of his hand, a command, to stay focused and follow their course.

She pressed him.

He held his gaze ahead.

Still, her eyes persisted his attention. *Your line is going to break, Yama!*

This thought peeled through his mind, extracted him away from his agenda— he became sharply aware of what she was thinking, as if a window was swung open into the directness of her mind.

"The Basin!" Yama responded aloud, thrusting his hand toward the head of the caravan.

She shouted back over the running thunder: "Stay tight!"

Dakkard noticed the conflict within the moment that it arose. "Shit of a time for that to happen!" He had been watching the heat rising between them for weeks. "Lover's quarrels," he would rasp, but keeping one eye always on them, waiting for the breaking point.

Dakkard had pulled out of line and topped a ridge, gaining him a view of the drop-ground. The basin was curved into a shallow horseshoe, dropping into a kind of shrub cloistered dike with deep walls of soil and stone, clamored with shrubbery, naked in the pre-spring colds.

As he continued to examine the land, a shagged form caught his eye, moving through the high witch reeds south of the drop-ground. "Great Mother," he cursed, lifting a brass scope to his eye, checking the reeds for certainty.

Kathrana was staring hard at Yama when she herd the shrill whistle slicing through distance behind them.

Yama looked past her, saw Darkkard waving his kerchief in the air.

They looked at each other with the alertness of danger, but they didn't miss a beat, suddenly quickened to a response— a new fear suddenly rippled through the herd.

Kathrana was first to see it— She cried out in her village-tongue "Maha Puchu!"

The Dengu Tiger approached with deliberate pace from the reeds, slinking his way into the exposed right-wing of the herd. He lunged into full gallop with an explosive burst, tackling a slow elder-bull, driving the rest of the herd into a rush of escape.

At the same time, Dakkard was watching the first of the bison dropping over the basin wall. Those bison who noticed the danger of the Tiger veered backward into the driving line of the Chasers. A giant bull bison doubled back, a young calf ran nervous, panicked, and scrambled under the stride of the bull. His knees buckled under two tons of momentum, colliding with the shale-turf beach at the edge of the basin, a spray of water pillowing off his mien.

Watching the bull fall caused the herd to fray across the basin's edge, fullstopping or sliding through the brittle chips of shale rock. Kathrana and Yama found themselves swept up under the sudden throwdown of the herd. Kathrana pulled back to a fullstop and readied her bow, noosing a long, thin arrow into the arch of her weapon.

She got a frantic scan of the situation: she saw Yama opening his stride and passing through a relative opening through the chaos. Then she got a flashing glimpse of the Tiger as it maneuvered through the trampling legs of the herd, shifting through the sparse grass.

He's causing a panic on purpose! she realized... *Hoping to break the herd apart to his advantage.*

As soon as the Tiger was gone from sight, the predator appeared again, slipping in and out of visibility this way, while the tremble of the bison spread itself thin along the basin's wall.

She sent an arrow singing through the skull of a heifer who had paralyzed itself with fear, standing dumb in the unsettling commotion. As it fell with dead weight into the grass, behind it, she saw a grinning face staring back at her.

"Pista!" she cried, as a tremble of fear reached into the roots of her beating heart, face to face with the Maha Puchu Tiger poised behind the fallen cow.

She knocked another arrow as the Tiger, unhurriedly, prowled past the bison, its gaze fixated on Kathrana.

Elem froze with fear, her silver eyes dilated with panic, her ears pivoted toward the silent stalking of the predator.

Kathrana's bow sprung an arrow in a timeless moment, hinged utterly on her ability to exact every molecule of her skill without the hesitation caused by trying—

Her shot planted itself into the slow ripple of the Tiger's shoulder. The animal shook with pain, lifted its great bearded neck and a base-level roar cascaded into the root of every beast, every man of the hunting party trembled, and Kathrana felt terror crawl up through the pith of her nature— walking the treacherous edges of her courage.

In the sudden moments after the herd was divided by the Tiger, Yama guided Drogo through a gap between the trampling beasts sprinted across the shale dirt, Drogo came to a fullstop and settled a meter from the basin wall. Yama glanced down into the basin, across the willows and the dwarf pines to where an ocean of grass lay beyond them. It was a beautiful view, he noticed, even in the after-wave of fear that was still turning through his mind.

He admired only an instant before a gut-wrenching roar turned his attention to the field. He felt the Tiger's presence warn every cell of his body, threaten his intelligence with an urge to run with dumb reaction.

He caught a blurry glimpse of Kathrana's bow arced at the end of her arm— his heart wanted to leap ahead of his body to protect her! But before his senses could respond, Yama was suddenly dwarfed below a sudden impact— the woolen wall of a bison's head plowed across Drogo's rump and threw both rider and animal spiraling apart.

Yama landed on the basin's edge and slid over the cleft of the breaking ground. As the bison scrambled over the same edge, the bull was plummeting just ahead of Yama, who was grappling with the wet snow for a limb to pull back from the fall… everything broke through his hands. It all unfolded in motion, the skidding of the rocks, the desperation— they plunged together over the basin.

When Yama came back to consciousness, he was already standing up. Before he could recognize any facet of his environment, before self-awareness returned, a dark mountain stood up behind him and sent him sprinting with an instinctual shock of agility.

A swift diving through the shrub brush told him exactly where he was… *inside the basin*. He had fallen in behind the bison. *He might have broken my fall*. Yama had the thought— but then he heard the sudden dropping of hooves. The bull drove through the barren witch reeds, bending willows beneath its chest. Yama was dancing away. Reeds hissing through the bison's stride, the wet slush of snow catching Yama as he leapt.

When the bull had turned about Yama was catching his breath. Both of them realized at the same time that the bison had frightened himself into a corner against the wall of the basin— he reacted immediately. Yama, with his own martial reaction, unsheathed his long-knife and set himself into poised defensive. The bull bison was staring at him with nervous attention.

With a forward throw of his head and a thumping front hoof, the bison levered his huge shoulders and lunged forward, breaking a causeway through the sedge and willows. In a swift flow to action, Yama dove aside where he could hide in the cover of dense bush.

The beast swung around. They faced each other. Yama danced to the high ground. The bull adjusted. His hoof pounded.

Suddenly, three arrows came whistling from above, penetrating the hump of the bull. He did not hesitate. In a throw of desperation the bull threw his might across the gap between them.

Yama threw his knife glinting through the rain. A sudden singing of arrows flurried into the dike. There was an abrupt collapse, a sudden drop in motion, and an elongated grunt ending with stillness.

Yama stood without moving. A castle of flesh lie at his feet. The great horns of the animal still moving, teetering, and finally rocking down to one side.

Yama noticed the rain falling on his bare forehead. *I lost my hat,* he thought.

"Are you hurt?" It was Dakkard's voice, from above.

Yama checked his hair for blood, felt his mouth for broken teeth, observed his hands: "I'm... I'm alright...!"

At the top of the basin wall several forms were staring down at him. One of them started a climb down.

Then Yama heard rustling in witch reeds... "Drogo!" he rushed. "Drogo, my friend." Yama found her further in the rear of the basin, lying over a bed of reeds and a broken left leg jutting out into bone. Yama's eyes filled with the hurt inside him, "I am sorry, my friend."

Kathrana came down the corridor of ditch wood with her bow over her shoulder and her cloak pulled tight. She was quickly at Yama's side. It was raining harder, the high wall of shale draining with fresh falling rain.

"That bull broke everything in your fall down the dike." said Kathrana.

Yama detected the anger she held toward him.

"Why did you rush for command of the chase when everything was going smooth?"

"It was a gut choice," said Yama.

"It was a stupid choice... everything was going easy. Why did you have to change that?"

"It was a tiger-attack, Kathrana! I couldn't have seen that coming!"

There was a quick silence. "The Tiger is dead," she said. Yama noticed her trembling; behind her eyes a trauma was fresh and remembering.

"Well… you'll get the profit." Yama turned away. He wanted to have his attention on Drogo.

Kathrana was struck by the gross distance in Yama's words, entirely out of tune with the battle she had just had with the Tiger, the unprocessed impact of the experience still sizzling within her. She clenched her jaw to stop a whiplash of anger…

Then she noticed Drogo lying in the reeds. Her anger went quiet. She felt an unexpected movement within her— she flinched with the urge to embrace him, comfort him. Love rushed forward. But she couldn't resist the urge to snap back into the pain they had caused each other. The unresolved below the surface pulling with a fierce gravity. She chose to suppress all feeling. Anger rolled back in: "You're going to have to shoot her," she said, biting her frustration.

Yama's heart began to burn. The rain was coiling down his face. He moved a little closer to the mare's side. His mind was suddenly on the battlefield again. The blood swelling into his skin. The overheated traces of fear. Pockets of anxiety collecting in his legs. Chewing tension in his jaws.

There was a sudden distance between he and Kathrana. He felt nothing for her. He only felt the rain, the shame pouring over him as he looked into the deep brown wells of Drogo's eyes.

"I cannot do this again," he said aloud.

"Do what?" Kathrana was sharp, loud, the rainfall clamoring and hissing through the dike.

"I can't be a part of the killing again. For the second time in my life I've made a profession of it... It ends here!"

"Yama, you know how we got here. Our choices put us into this position. Yours and Mine. There are some things we just have to do— and you need to put Drogo down... she's waiting."

His heart sank into bitterness for Kathrana.

Yama felt the fear of not being understood... but he knew she was right... "Give me your bow."

She handed him the bow with two arrows. "Make it quick, I'm going to start skinning this one." And she made her way to the bull's corpse.

Yama walked to Drogo's side. She was still and breathing steadily. "I have seen many friends killed, Drogo..." He knocked the arrow. "To many I owe my own life... and theirs they owe to me. You and I were friends, no man could doubt it... But violence has a different way than the friendships of men— and I've become certain, Drogo, it is no way to live a life... this is the lesson you give to me this day."

Yama pulled the bow taught. He paused, his middle finger betraying a quiver of strength from his arm, and not until the arrow loosed on its own accord, did the arrow fly. It pierced through Drogo and he fell, quivering to stillness.

"That was it, then." And his words were hard and distant.

"Yama…" Kathrana called him.

Yama joined her. "Please hold the skin." She said, a knife glittering through red flesh. "Come on, Yama. If we don't skin we don't eat. That's the way of it. Please." And she gestured to the loose hide peeled back from the shoulder.

"I once saw thirty men slaughtered by the same weapon, in a single instant. I still remember the pools of blood and flashing of light… The horror of it was blinding… What have we become, Kathrana? "

"Nothing, Yama! We are nothing…please, I need your help with this."

"I can't do this anymore, Kathrana!"

"But that won't stop you!" Kathrana's eyes were darting through the rain at him. "Because if you want to move south, if you want to run away, then we need to fucking eat.."

"Why are we taking these skins back for money? Why don't we eat the animals… we killed them."

"Fine! Go make a goddam fire!" She knelt and continued to peel back the sleeve of the bison's leg, the rain falling harder.

Yama suddenly felt empty. Rain was pouring through the dike. Water was gathering around them. The neck of their boots wading.

By impulse, Yama walked to Kathrana's side.

"Yama," she turned to him and stood to look him into the eyes. "When we set-out together, your first promise was to carry your own weight…" She held up a knife blade, rain drizzling through the blood at its edges. "Please, I need you to carry it—" and her voice ended with a clear line— and she invited him to choose a side.

He paused, aware of the choice in front of him. Love flooded forward in his heart. He couldn't deny it. He didn't want to love her— but he did. No part of him wanted to continue. His oath to Drogo would be honored… however, one piece of himself remained in-love with Kathrana…

No one who has ever loved can pin a truth on exactly why any man makes the choice Yama made… even though he felt the gravity of desolation within him, he looked at Kathrana through the anger moving in her eyes, and saw love inside himself— raising his palm to his forehead and to the heart, he spoke in the words of Kathrana's village-tongue: "Depoah Manu…"

Kathrana took a deep breath, remembering the words of the Gwen Eden, spoken to her years ago in her home-village… She closed her eyes. Opened them again— Yama took a deep breath and received the knife into his hand.

Heartsword

When the path grows difficult
I become a cloud casting rocks
I retreat into dense earth, packed
and stoned into deserts and mountains
until my neighbors become foreigners
and friends strange beggars.
Lightning never struck such a wondrous fear
as the unknown.
The Sun never dispelled such a lovely darkness
as the nights we've been alone.
As old as any Soul remembers
we have unlearned lessons pouring our sorrows
into heartbreak's poor broken cups.
I could only hear what I wanted to hear
my thirst was following a sweetness
in the sound of water.
The mistakes have been my own—
from this glitter of silver
I sold all my belongings for a dream of treasure.
What happens to a Man who misread Himself
and stumbles into a dark meadow?

Someone has been teaching birdsongs to the wolves.

There are teeth waiting in the grass.

His heart quivers in his hands

but a moment is coming

that will awaken both edges of his sword.

Yesterdays of Bliss

Where do we go from here?

Decisions are to be made.

Money earned.

Relationships are waiting

for our needs to reveal themselves.

What was bliss one night

becomes pain another day.

What was once union

divides into continents of war.

Where is freedom, really?

Inside the emotional heart of a lover?

Inside a throbbing body, opening?

Perhaps our sense of self is found

standing alone, above the world, mountainous?

Or we find ourselves in the gunfire of a nation

breaking free from the shackles of prejudice?

Perhaps your freedom is not popular to anyone else.

Maybe it will be found at the bottom of a foolish project...

what's my point?

I'm trying to speak a truth
but my mouth is too clumsy
to tell you.
I know we both must leave this place
someday. You are not my Truth.
We all have different paths
like water down the side of a mountain
we carve our own way through the roots of life.

At some point we'll meet again
when all these different paths unite...
we'll meet again, my love,
but not like this
not like this.

Roots

Yet again, we must change our footing—

as she does

the Earth has moved like a dancer around us.

I begin to think we are not designed

for the bedrock of this world

constant motion

always keeping our roots dry.

We thought we arrived at a plateau of stone

instead, we were born into an ocean.

Regardless if life brings you

the many fashions of love

or a renaissance of anger—

even if you are greeted

by the peacekeeping of a foreign tongue

or terrorism in your own house

be prepared

because what you see is *Yourself*

troughing through the shadow

of another

oncoming wave.

A Fire Within

If I'm going to write poetry

I'm done speaking sweetly.

Words are all too delicate

for life. And Humans

are all too careless with words.

Inner knowing speaks

with the rugged realities

of our actions.

Poets are not offering you anything

of real substance. Do you feel cheated?

Do you want to ask me why

the hell you are still reading?

Because

we are all in the wild, searching

for a map to mark our place in life.

Because we smell a beast in the shadows

and we're foraging for protection.

My words are merely a temporary shelter.

A coat you found on an empty night.

Take the contents of this raw

woven rug of meanings

and sleep on it when there is nothing

between you

and the ground that wants to bury you.

Use it for prayer

if that's what keeps you warm at night.

But for god's sake

don't stay long—

keep moving towards the fire

that inspires you.

Rough and Narrow

What was our truth today

becomes our spinning confusion tomorrow.

What seemed to be right action

stirs up a nest of mistrust in our hearts.

If there was a ring of keys

for every interaction between two

hearts in love,

then Truth must know our every corridor

warden of the rooms between us.

I wish I knew how to tell you

the ways to uncover dark windows

and wells of fearful stairs

that awaits those who undertake this imperfect path

of loving another person.

I beg for the quake of understanding

that breaks a crack in the labyrinth.

I pray these stones below my knees

may soften

the way two people who are in love

have ever softening eyes for each other.

Yet once we find Truth and pin her to our hearts

she has already escaped our grasp

and moved-on down our paths.

So hopeful is that single, penetrating

glance of freedom

that we'd do it all again

for another ten-thousand square miles

of rough and narrow inspiration.

Beloved Freedom

I want to know my own freedom

somewhere between the muscles of the horse

and the grass— where he is infinite.

I want to know the pounding heart

and the beating wing

where we flock as one, great mind.

I want to know my own thoughts

as deep as the thighs

of my lover... even deeper.

There are stories of women

who loved so fiercely

that they ruled the world

from inside the bed chambers of Kings.

Stories of women

who stood beside an Emperor

and broke the bondage of his heart

even after his armies brought her

to his house

in chains.

Women who cut the crown

from their hair— abandoned it

as hungry as a desert bush

sleeping with the wolves at night

with a vow in their hearts

never to weep again

at the windows of towers.

To know that kind of spirit

what man wouldn't attempt

to shape the sands of his poorest desert

into a megalith of time?

What man wouldn't flagstaff

the dark side of a planet

or split the particles of his desire

For a beloved

who would show him his own freedom

somewhere between

the question

and the secret in her face?

The Archer

The archer holds his arrow

in precious tension with the bow.

The feather on his cheek, a sweet remembering

of the shot that once pierced his heart—

that white bison that fell at the foot of his soul

the thundering buffalo of his desire

in the restless grass of his wild mind.

The Arrow, all that he Is, His Center

pinned between two fingers

he waits for that spontaneous surrender

when the bow releases

an ecstatic song through her forest branches

a penetration that brings him to his knees

a love made in the pith of their bodies.

The beast of this Ego

wanes in leaves of autumn

our passion turns into moons.

You came with baskets, picking ears of corn

from the trembling of my heart.

I went far and wide

looking for you.

There is a game about our loving

that nature insists.

Creature hunts creature.

Mates must dance for what they find.

And for all the hunts of Man and Woman

there is an Arrow knocked to our Being

and there is a Death

at the end of our Path.

Without Conditions

A love that sharpens me as a person

is a love that I can respect.

This is not a warm bed

or the comfort of bridal promises.

Our gardens are grown in torn soil

Sprouts will find imperfect routes

to escape dense earth.

The point isn't to secure

a state of perfect caring...

Love, at her finest,

will train you with defiance

in order to show you compassion

without conditions.

Cob Mosque

There must be a transformative nature.

Something that can give us courage

through the back-waters of Samskara— a lantern

through those nightlong searches for a dream.

We seek a place where we are individuals.

Where we are Islands.

Where we are Kings.

Then we build our castles out of the relationships around

us...

But Soul cannot become clay.

Love is too curious and free

to become mortar in a wall.

A poet of the Heart

must understand his road

has many companions

and fills his wounds wherever Love

is offering medicine.

There are no shelters of this world

which offer comfort forever.

Just as soon as we find

what we are looking for— the roof

gets pulled from across our head. We depart

another house of healing.

We settle our debts

at another burlesque of truth.

We must keep moving.

And for those times, lonesome

on a trail below the stars—

we remember the households of our friends...

And when we are stranded

in the boondocks of unworthiness

enter the humble cob mosque of your heart

and Pray— remembering

that your Path has been

your greatest Home.

4.
<u>Final Scene</u>

Prayer flags hung in a small tree

Soft threads unwoven

Mountain wind pulling them free

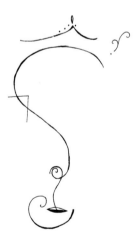

Passage of the Bichwour Wastes

Yama removed his slippers at the door of the mosque and then entered. The fluttering of candles burned warm along the cob walls. Along the mantle of a simple, white alter, an oil joyti burned, its light clapping against the back of the wall. At its base was the single, undying blossom of a dragon flower, perched in a mala of Rheda seeds. Behind it, the simple form of a supple-faced figure, sitting in lotus, hands resting on his robe.

Yama approached the altar and lowered himself to a rug on the floor. Once bowing, he stood again and lay a small wooden box on the mantle. He removed a small set of bamboo tweezers, a cotton wick, a bottle of golden oil... carefully, with meditative attention, he tended to the delicate wick of the jhoti. He adjusted his sleeve away from his hand. With the tweezers, he pulled the shortened wick further out the oil in the basin. The flame flickered higher. His shawl gently fell from his shoulder. With intentional slowness, he replaced it around his collar. He removed the cork from the bottle and poured oil into the lamp. He tinkered with the wick, adjusting the height of the flame.

Through the corner of his eye he noticed a shadow cross the sunlight which lay across the floor from the doorway. He felt a presence behind him. The rush of a robe coming to stillness.

"Someone has come…" said the voice of a young boy. "She says you are friends."

Yama's heart suddenly trembled. The flame of the jhoti dashed. Candles along the west wall whispered. "Thank you, Kepla."

The boy hurried away.

Yama completed his task unhurriedly, attentively collecting his tools and closing them into the box. He stepped back, lowered himself to the rug, stood again and did not turn from the altar until his feet were touching the earthen floor outside the altar's presence.

Now his heart was racing. He tossed his shawl over his shoulder, picked up a corner of his robe and rushed outside.

Yama followed a cobbled pathway down a high ridge, green grass flowing over a short wall, weeping willows unfurling their skirts into the mountain wind. After short descent of steps he came to a platform at the doorstep of a small earthen hut. From the low, dark doorway, Kepla came scuttling across the doormat with a jug of water, his eyes looking up at Yama like a mouse who didn't expect to see anyone.

"Your friend is thirsty."

"Take me to her, Kepla."

He followed the young boy, shaven head, ears that pedaled forward like two flowers, anxious strides below his robe. He led Yama down a throughway with a high wall, grass hanging down from the hillside, whispering across the masonry. Another set of stairs, rocks fitted into the raw dirt lead them around a tall embankment to the threshold of a stone spire. The face of the watchman leaned over a high windowsill as they passed below. The trail was taking them ever lower down the mountain's steep ridge. Yama leaned over the short wall, no higher than his hip, for a view of patchwork of rooftops below, built into the joint of two mighty mountainsides. Where the two slopes joined, a swift stream ran, flowing beneath the stone-made plaza and jutting with a brave and bottomless dive over the pine-trees rooted far below the ridgetops.

Kepla moved across the uneven step-work without spilling a drop of water from the basin which he held firmly in his arms. The tail of his robe was dirty, kicking pebbles, his sandals brushing the path.

Once entering the plaza, there was the movement of people, robes swishing with busyness. Sanyas were sweeping the stones and stairways, goats were feeding from the stable corners, baying with laughter, crows cried from dwarfed pines on the grassy, upper slopes.

Yama noticed bedding being carried into a hut, a large blanket and grass pillow- *That would be for our guest*, he thought- And his heart leapt with anxious possibility.

Along the stiff bank of the steep ridge were constructed many earthen buildings, meager in their necessities, but hardy enough to exist a community of esthetics and the seasonal roar of mountain winds. In a small alcove flourished a dense garden, a single bench sat below a simple outcropping of stone, a meditating sculpture hidden in the depth of flowers.

"She was just here," said Kepla, approaching the bench and resting his load of water onto it. "I told her to stay."

"It's alright, Kepla. Bring cups."

He swiftly hurried away.

Yama took a deep breath. The smell of dank running water filled him. The air was cool with spring.

"Hello, Yama."

The voice penetrated him with knowing. An instant, cutting recognition spun Yama around, his shawl slipping off his shoulder. "Kathrana... somehow I knew it was you."

She smiled, letting their eyes linger on each other a moment. Then she spoke: "I've come a long way... I'm sure my presence is a strange occurrence in this place... I hope it is no trouble for you."

"We share our troubles here... and our friends... you are welcome."

"Hept Ahoah," she greeted him in her village-tongue.

"Nu Mani Om," he said in tradition of his community.

They lingered in silence. The patient movement of daily work around them.

Kepla returned and placed two clay cups beside the basin. His eyes looked warily at the foreigner. She smiled at him.

"Kathrana and I have been friends a long time," Yama said to the boy. "Please go and inform Anishtabav to add one more for evening meal"

The boy leapt to obey.

"Thank you," Kathrana spoke swiftly and gratefully.

Yama noted the earnestness in her response. "And Kepla," the boy scurried back. "Bring some bread from the kitchen." The boy bowed and dashed away.

"Thank you, Yama."

Yama took a cup and filled it with water, handed it to her. "I've some duties to attend to, but this evening there will a space for us to share."

"Won't you stay for a drink?" She gestured to the empty cup on the bench.

Yama's heart was pounding. He focused on his breathing. But his chest was surging. "I had better go, for now. Meals are eaten in silence. After evening clean-up you may want to rest. I will check to make sure you're comfortable."

Yama could see the confused disappointment in her eyes.

"I will return to make sure you are comfortable." And then Yama, robe swishing against the smooth stones, crossed the courtyard with hasty steps.

Kathrana watched him walk away. She finished her water and by this time Kepla returned with bread wrapped in cloth. He held the loaf in his arms and led her to her private quarters before dinner.

Later that evening, Kathrana was wearing the robe she found laid over her bed, appreciating the smooth fabric against her slender frame. She was feeling satisfied by a dinner of hot soup and half the loaf of sourdough bread Kepla left her with after introducing her to her room. She was looking into the still water of a basin in her quarters, combing her hair, noticing the matured lines in her face, sharpened by five years of living from the hand of the world.

A knock tapped at the door- "Yes?"

"It's me," said the visitor.

"Come in, Yama." Kathrana lay the comb beside the basin.

The small door, made of light pine, swung open, outlined by a single lantern held in Yama's hand. "I've come to see if you are comfortable." He said from the doorway.

"Yes, I am, thank you." Kathrana turned to face him. Yama remained outside, his presence reserved at the doorsill. "Won't you come in, Yama?"

"It may be best if we talk tomorrow."

Kathrana grabbed the side of her robe and sighed- "I've come a long way... Speak to me, Yama."

He lingered in reluctant silence. "It is not appropriate for me to enter a woman's private quarters."

"There must be another place?"

Again, Yama fell quiet. After some reluctance he spoke: "Yes... follow me."

They came to a quiet courtyard under open sky. It was dark as they entered, but, one by one, Yama dutifully lit a series of candles along one of the inner walls. Taking one of the candlesticks, he tenderly protected its flame as he carried it across the stone floor and ignited lanterns at the open balcony.

With a well-lit room, Kathrana could see Yama with some clarity; his robe was green and lined with a crimson seam, his head was newly shaved, the lack of a tan-line indicating he has worn his hair in this fashion for some time, and his sandals lightly brushed the floor as he carefully poured two glasses of water.

"This is the contemplation courtyard," Yama delivered Kathrana her cup, his eyes averting hers. "It is intended to be a silent space, however, I've been given admittance to speak to you here."

"You live a formal life here," said Kathrana, trying to catch his gaze as he studied the room around them.

"It's a place of simple reverence." Then Yama turned his gaze to finally meet the eyes of his past lover— "Kathrana, what have you come to say?"

The intensity in his eyes was hard to look at... She turned and walked to the balcony, looked up at the mountainsides of pine spread at the feet of the mosque. Her hand touched the banister of the balcony, green blades of grass growing to its edges. She was withdrawn, her eyes barely open.

"I love the smell of the pine." She smiled- "It reminds me of my birth-land... we lived under the Gendo Popeho Mountain, a rich skirt of pine covered her basin. Her glaciers would glitter in the full day sun. Wind would brush the pine forests every night. I slept every night with that hushing music outside. Whippoorwills called deep in the night— I use to think they were lonely."

" 'To be like the Whippoorwill, to be lonesome, is to sing in the dark while the world fights in their sleep.' "

"Did you write that?"

"It's an idiom of our teachings," Yama said as he found a seat on a mat near the center garden of the courtyard.

Kathrana sighed and turned her head gently to the west. "My people had no enemies. We had good friends. We were safe there... a place confronted with the wild around us, but danger's hand never reached my bedside. I was truly free to grow."

Yama's robe was warm in the candlelight where he sat. "I've never heard you speak so fondly of your birth-village."

She nodded at his awareness. "I went back."

Yama picked himself off the rug and eagerly joined her at the banister.

Kathrana continued to speak: "I'm not quite sure what compelled me to do it. But when we left each other in Dimroh, I paid for supplies and took the road west..."

"You didn't go by ship?"

"Ney... big waters never suited me."

"There is no trail west except the lumber corridor— The Bichwour Waste..."

"The mud turns silver at night," the corners of Kathrana's eyes were smiling. "A result of the heavy minerals washing down from the mining at high elevations."

"But that causeway is cursed."

"Not cursed, Yama... *inhabited*."

"Nevertheless, very dangerous."

"It was my path..."

A quiet moment fell between them. They looked out at the gentle night as they listened to the pines sway.

"You are a woman, traveling toward the mining sietches of lawless men... how did you conceal yourself from the Kaboah Workers?"

"In the mining town of Dwelsh I came to the Watership Inn, dressed as a man. I cut my hair, changed my voice and never walked in the streets with my hood down. My hands were already so rough from hunting the bison. They were already trained for the knife. So everything I touched had a hint of confidence that would be expected of a man."

"Did you take the causeway alone?"

"The Inn was occupied by a crowd of stoic men. The fireplace was already burning when I arrived early in the morning. I ordered a loaf of bread and cheese, and the Inn-attendant told me the party at the tables behind me were leaving for the Bichwour on the morning of the next day. I paid him an extra coin for the bread. I knew I had to take up travel with this party of workers... but I would also have to conceal the fact that I was a woman. I was terrified."

Yama was resting his hip against the banister, observing Kathrana- the softness behind her ears, the angular collar of her green tunic, sandy hair barely touching the short point in her ears, trimmed short at the back of the neck. "Were you ever discovered?"

"There was one man who suspected me..."

Yama noticed Kathrana's tone and posture suddenly change- "I would like to tell you the story..."

"His name was Rowland, a strider from the outer rims of the Empire. He made a living as a Hound Martial, master of three, massive, Kuwado Dogs. The workers called them dire dogs. Rowland is hired to command the animals for protection of caravans on perilous journeys... The first time I saw them, they stood in the tall grass where the caravan had gathered in a field prior to departure.

The massive head of the lead dog watched me approach the caravan as they organized equipment for departure. Standing nearly to my elbows, with a back as wide as a horse, his pink, half-cone ears pivoted with interest toward me. I froze with unexpected fear as his eyes pierced me from inside his wide skull.

'Don't be afraid...' said Rowland, saddling a mule with gear. 'He knew you were coming before you entered the field.'

My fear softened, knowing Rowland was there... 'His name is Kualu,"'he motioned to the dog, closing the flap of his saddlebag and kneeling to the dog's side, brushing his deep, muscular-set shoulder.

Suddenly another dog reared its powerful back out of the grass and joined Rowland's side. Both hounds stood every bit as tall as the mule. 'This one is named Archu—' he said, giving him a rub through his thick, bearded chest. Built a bit smaller than Kualu, but no less endowed with the characteristic muscle-power and deep-set structure of dogs that were bred to stand ground against the paleo animals of the wilds.

'We have been partners for many years...' Both dogs stood with possessive respect of Rowland, their broad noses scanning the environment, wide framed jaws set with bone-breaking potential. Archu brushed his head against Rowland, stood a step closer to him, comforted by the love of his master.

'They are both proud males,' I said in observation.

The alpha, Kualu, stood at Rowlands arm, guarded, alert, poised in a shielding stance- 'They are honorable friends.' He gave Kualu a strong pat against the shoulder.

Then Rowland had a look around the grounds where the caravan was gathered, finishing up preparations. The tall grass swayed around the hips of the grazing horses. The grounds were trampled into a mat of grass packed below the feet of the loitering caravan. Rowland's eyes searched through the edges of the field— then he gave a shrill whistle that went in all directions. Heads turned from their provisions, paused, and then returned to their business.

After only a few beats, the grass parted from the edge of the camp and the broad strength of a silver wolf danced to Rowland's side. Her eyes were scarlet, hinted with bronze lines, black eyelids framing each round of a piercing pupil that could seize you in a kind of spiritual stillness. My breath gave way as she gazed over me.

'This is Mincha... the only lady amongst us...'

Rowland didn't catch me blushing. I quickly responded, but as I revisited the wolf's gaze, I was taken aback... 'Her eyes—' I stumbled. 'Were they always blue?'

Rowland smiled, amused by the familiar game. 'Beautiful, like glaciers, aren't they?'

I shook my head- 'they were only a moment ago, scarlet, like blood on a rusting sword.'

'Yes, great description,' he said, a smirk curling at the ends of his mouth.

'Are we talking about the same thing here?'

Rowland stood and laughed. 'Dire breeds, like Mincha, have changing eye colors. It is a genetic trait of Mannah, or energy. I have witnessed her eyes change into many expressions, like ferocity or bonding... but when her eyes turn blue like this, I think she is seeing something that the rest of us cannot see, looking into a realm beyond our human eyes.'

This wolf held me in her gaze, bewitched by the eyes— I was held in the frozen blue depths that sent chills through the deep waters of my soul.

Suddenly her eyes snapped to a dark, pollen yellow, and her attention was drawn by motions of the onset from the caravan- "We're leaving..." And Rowland stood- "What is your name, friend?"

'Puro... from the boarder villages of the Wilding Plains.'

'I see...' and then he turned to walk away, the dogs following close inside his wing, a Sherpa picking up the reins of the donkey and guiding it toward an assembly of animals. The rest of us followed the lead of the Trailheader, a man named Dokada, who was aiming us west into the diving footsteps of the Puhgamu Alps."

Yama suddenly stood and approached the altar to relight some candles that blew out in the gradual breeze of their evening. In his hand, he was counting mantra with mala beads, his shoulders slightly rounded, holding some emotion. "You say this man discovered you... How?"

"He caught me alone one night. I had grown a rash on my inner thigh and I had been ignoring its treatment. He approached me as I was rubbing the rash with a poultice- 'This is a brave journey for you,' he interrupted.

My heart nearly leapt out of my shirt, pulling the fly of my trousers closed, wiping poultice across my shirt-sleeve.

He stepped to my side in a confident stride and a slow, deliberate bend to his knees, opening his wool trenchcoat with a slow, calculated bend to his knees- 'First time through the Bichwour is a defining passage. You will encounter fear that you've never imagined.'

After all I had seen in previous years, I laughed at his comment.

'There will be no fires at night...' Rowland continued. 'Every night we make camp, we will set-up our mats together, in a circle, with our luggage placed in the center of camp. Keep your weapon at your side and engaged. Do not wander to relieve yourself after hours. There will be a watchman and you will be asked to take shifts. Manage your sleep. Do not interfere with the pace of the party; that is set by the work-team. We are only with them for the safety of our numbers. They have no obligation to us...'

'What is the danger of lighting a fire?'

'We can light fires by day. We will do all our cooking in the evening before sunset. By night, not even an ember can glow...'

Laughter came from camp. Some of the workers staying up late. Their voices disappearing into the low darkness.

'We are safer in the darkness?'

'Light in the Bichwour brings something worse than the darkness.'

'If you have a warning for me, Rowland, say it outright—'

'I am informing you...' He spoke with compassionate directness. 'This party will leave you alone in the lumber wastes if you betray your secret... Draw too much attention to yourself and they will see what I see.'

'There is nothing to see.'

Rowland's eyes narrowed on her- 'There is a full moon in two days...'

Kathrana's brow bent with interest. 'Moonlight brings more danger?'

Rowland's head nodded. 'For you, yes... it is your time to bleed. I wanted to be the first one to find you. Don't allow the other men to find you as I have. They will take you. If you kill one of them in defense, it will cause you trouble you cannot handle. You'll have no choice. They will take you.'

I was brought to silence with fear. I was looking into the deep bed of the forest floor, trying to avoid any disturbance by the images triggered by Rowland's warning, bending my mind to focus on anything else, anything but the fear.

'So what's your real name?' Rowland asked.

I hesitated, but knew it was useless. 'Kathrana.'

He nodded and smiled.

'Will you tell me what keeps us hiding in the dark? What makes a team of able men sleep, cuddling in fear?'

'You misunderstand these men…' Rowland touched the end of his coat, casually plucking a loose string from the hem. 'They are roughnecks…' Rowland was smiling. 'But they are not fools. If you want to survive, go unnoticed, if you can, follow closely, and do not burn light after dark… it is more important than you know.'

'There is something in the Bichwour— you will leave me ignorant?'

'Now you know enough… I pray you do not have a chance to see what the light brings.'"

"This man, he spared you and your secret… Why?" Yama was holding a string rolled in incense resin, a lick of flame at its end producing a milky coil of smoke.

Kathrana was looking at a star low in the sky, dangling at the swaying edges of the pine forest that grew against the steep shelves surrounding the temple. It trembled there between the fray of wind-combed dwarf cedar and white pine. A blue light was rising, cool and watery behind the slender curves of the high ranges. "Because his destination lay at the other side of the Bichwour. He needed to get across the wastes. He was intelligent. He took me on as a friend, but all the while, if I crossed him, he held a secret to yield me."

"He was using you."

Kathrana suppressed a flash of anger at the statement: "The Kaboah Workers were not so different from the smugglers in the Wilding Plains… however, the smugglers were focused on a profit. That profit kept them alert. The Kaboah were men of work. They lived with hardship. Their relief was belligerence. That fact made them all the more dangerous. A sober partner made all the difference. This was why Rowland sympathized with my secret."

"He was holding a secret too… what was he withholding about the dangers of the Bichwour?"

Kathrana went quiet. Her gaze grew heavy on the slow brightness growing on the horizon.

"On the third night, I was lying down, a blanket pulled over my shoulders. We had just stamped out the fire from dinner and the others were laying out their bedmats. The moon rose quickly, the east softening with a gradual, milky darkness. That's when, deep in the wood-wastes, a shredding cry carried over the distance. The sound was strange. I didn't understand what I was hearing. Later I realized that the cry of this creature did not echo, as if it were a sound without vibration, a voice without life. It had a dead quality in it, yet, piercing the roots within me.

The camp went quiet and still. The workers quickly stamped out their cigarettes, not to risk the light which was stoked from inhales.

I leaned over to Rowland, who made his bed beside me: 'When do I need to worry about that sound?'

Rowland spoke softly, his hand on Kualu's back as the dog gazed forward into the night with rasied ears, a low snarl in his throat- 'When you see it,' said Rowland. 'It is already hunting you.'

I wanted to ask him more questions, but when I opened my mouth to speak again, he made a gesture to quiet me. I quieted my concerns... night was coming quickly now and the eastern darkness began to unfold with its milky glow."

"It is no small feat to silence you when you have mind to speak," Yama was grinning.

Kathrana returned him a humored glare, a smile opened to edges of her face. Then she turned away from him- "I pulled my bow and quiver close to me that evening as I lay down to close my eyes. I felt secure enough with Rowland... I felt stable there with him."

Yama's undercurrent of reserve grew deeper. His eyes fell away from her. Kathrana hesitated, seeing the change in him, and then she continued...

"I sat back quietly and looked up at the sky. The starless night washed in the light of Enyana, glittering in the distance beyond the foothills. I thought of you in that moment, and in the quiet worry of those nights, I thought of our times together."

Yama closed his hands together in his lap, looked away at the edge of the floor- "I've thought often of our nights under the stars, making love, exploring each other in body and conversations..."

Kathrana felt something coming from him, the carefully unexpressed emotion, betrayed so slightly in a sense of reserve in his posture. She remained steady in her gaze, watching the emotion agitate his mannerisms

Yama spoke with his face lowing toward the gorge far below the Temple: "Did you encounter the danger? Did you see the creature worse than darkness?"

Kathrana lowered her head: "Yes..."

"Late in the night I was awoken to some commotion.

I saw Rowland rushing toward the hearth. He was desperately kicking a log out of the coals. The watchman had fallen asleep on his shift and the wind had blown fresh flames out of the embers without our knowing. Rowland suddenly faded into shadow as he dropped a heavy blanket over the flames, submitting the light— in that moment the moon peaked over the hillsides, a scarlet faced moonlight, followed by a wild and wrenching cry passing through the Bichwour with an echoless ether.

'We're too late?' said Rowland, looking out across the silver dunes of mud and litter of lumber wastes. A second cry swept across the wasteland. Rowland's face darkened.

I lifted myself out of my blanket- 'Are we in danger?'

Rowland made eye contact with me. He held it a long time. I felt fear rise up inside my heart...

By the next morning we were five days deep into the wastes. Sound of the wraiths the night before left everyone in a somber mood. Everyone was walking with a clip in their steps, thoughts of the safe sietches, still many days away.

We came to an area that permitted some swampish plant-life to grow. Course reeds and cattail filled a low sink of wet ground. As we tread the outside of the small bog, a family of sycamore grew tight against its edges, brushing each other in the wind.

As our trail widened it led up a short hill into a higher meadow growing scant tufts of grass and scrawny growths of yucca. Before we reached the top, I felt the thrilling tingle of fear as the Kuwado Hounds started barking, unseen over the edge of the slope.

Rowland was close and his command echoed across the hillsides: 'Hold!'

I rushed to the hilltop with a full back of luggage. I saw Rowland standing firm with a wall of reed grass to his right. To the left was a wide ground of malnourished soil. The dire-dogs were standing in form, frozen under Rowland's command, their eyes fixated ahead into the heaps of clear-cut waste.

I shouldered my pack to the ground and stood watchfully- Rowland's eyes were hard, examining the landscape, his whip unrolled at his feet— the dogs were snarling, deep, pithy rumbles in their throats— Mincha's eyes blazing as blue as frozen lakes.

Dokada strode with heavy boots to Rowland's left side- 'What's happening?'

'She sees it,' I overheard Rowland say.

'What is it?'

'A wraith...'

My blood went chilled. I tried to deny what I heard.

Rowland was grim, his eyes serious and searching the hillsides.

'Be wary, friend,' said Dokada sternly. 'A claim like that could unnerve the entire party. There are many beasts in these lands. Do you see a shadow and imagine a devil?'

'I know what I saw.'

'I thought they only hunt at night?' said Dokada.

'That is true,' Rowland was eyeing the slopes ahead. 'But they still move through the day...They will only take you in your sleep... They hunt in your dreams.'

A shiver crawled up my spine. I wrapped my arms around my chest. A chilled wind blew down from the high peaks.

'We are being stalked.'

Dokada looked back at his caravan who stood at the crest of the hillside watching them.

'Take care of this now, Rowland... this is what I hired you for.'

Rowland grew heavy with Dokada's suggestion. He looked at his Kuwado. Now the dogs looked back at Rowland. Their waiting didn't betray anxiety— rather, a pin-pointed control of urges, a thoroughly refined selection of primitive nature that was completely loyal to Rowland's voice. Their temperament was plated below rigorous training in which they were conditioned to pose no contest to their escort, especially their master. Rowland stood in their presence as a commander, unshakable, composed with sureness, clarity— he held himself as if he had never been broken... he did not succumb to intimidation under any circumstance. The dogs sensed his presence and respected it.

Rowland's eyes met them. There was a hanging pause in the situation held entirely in Rowlands command. His next action was swift and firm. He raised his hand with a quick sweep and the crack of his whip, followed by a sharp snap of instruction, a word developed only between he and the dogs, a command delivered to kill.

Kualu was first to launch from his place. The other two followed with muscles rippling. They dove through a patch of reed and emerged out the other side moving twice the speed, charging around a mound of wood waste and down a swift slope.

Talk quickly ran through the caravan. The men were crowding forward for a better view, excitement bristling, captive by the instant release of anticipation.

We heard barking from the other side of the hill. *They found it*, I thought. My heart was racing.

Suddenly, a wide and brown creature emerged from the waste. A bewildered pause fell over Rowland as the unexpected animal rounded over the slope, followed closely by the Kuwado and it's heels.

A Bull Elk rumbled into the barren meadow, stopped ahead of the reeds, revealing a wide breadth of white chest, long muscles stretching below his thick fur into the knobby knees and slip-toe hooves of his legs. The Bull shook his rack, clattering against a nearby sycamore, followed by extending his neck and letting out a swift bellow into the hills.

'Yield!' Rowland commanded. 'Leave it!' But it was too late. The dogs were heated by the conflict, the bull also, livid with aggression, pivoted headlong, spread his legs wide, dropping his rack down into forward view. I was agape at his size.

The dogs spread wide around the Elk. Kualu stopping at the animal's face, jaws snapping, lips furled back to an open pair of teeth. The other two circled around the animal. The bull rushed with its antlers. Kualu dodged, barking furiously, skidding past the wide ends of the mantle by a tail's length.

Archu came around from the left side and snapped at the animal's legs. Mincha was circling, biting the back legs and fending hard kicks. As the other two put the pressure on the animal, Kualu bolted, ramped forward and latched his jaws around the Elk's muzzle.

The huge rack of antlers shook as the square head bucked side to side, giving Kualu two wide swings before, with impressive motion, catapulting him, legs wading airborne across the meadow.

I watched him fall into the high grass. I thought the dog would have been dead. But the grass shook and out came the bruised but haughty predator in full stride, with pounding speed, running across the gap to rejoin the attack.

The other two, Archu and Mincha, were backing the Elk into a pocket of rock, taking bites at the legs. The alpha rejoined the attack with a dynamic headlong dive onto the Elk's left-side, sinking his jaws around the lean meat of his shoulder. The sheer weight behind the attack brought the Elk into a stumble, rocking backwards with his hooves tripping through the stones.

This moment encouraged the other dogs to take leaps. Archu leapt from the high ground onto the Elk's back and buried his jaw around its hump. The animal staggered, backed himself against a slope and fell in desperate recovery.

Mincha made a direct lunge for the neck as the bull was coming down. Archu made a hard fall to the ground while the Kualu fell from the shoulder in a controlled dive. Both immediately regained themselves and sunk their snarling faces deep into the mountain of fur while Mincha gripped it under the soft flesh of the neck.

It didn't take long before there was no more sign of struggle from the Elk. All three dogs waited, teeth deep inside the animal, their ribs pulsing with hard breaths.

Once the fight was finished, Rowland cracked his whip and approached the kill with wide strides. The dogs were still riled by the fight, so he cracked his whip at their backside to get their attention and moved forward to claim the kill.

Dokada waited for Rowland to look back. He approached the massive body of the Elk where Rowland stood, the dogs wide-eyed and fixated on the taste of blood on their chops.

'A wraith, aye?' He scolded.

Rowland swallowed his pride.

'We have four more days before we reach the first sietch,' Dokada was close to Rowland, speaking into his ear. We don't need false fears undermining the integrity of this caravan. You have made many journeys through these lands, Rowland, and my respect for your survival is the only grace between us. But the life of these men are in my hands. There are other martials for hire in these lands. Do not allow your fear to compromise this mission again. Understood?'

Rowland was quiet for a moment, controlling his anger with stoic repose, and then he acknowledged the command with a subtle, forced nod of the head."

It was growing late for Kathrana and Yama... The moonlight was dipping low against the earthen architecture of the temple, the last candle had been dowsed in the windows, leaving only the contemplation hall still warmly wrapped in light. Yama was standing in front of the garden with his hands behind his back, the gentle fountain trembling through the broad-leaf ferns and thorny flowers.

"Kathrana I have to say something..."

She joined him at the edge of the vegetation, cool moonlight glancing toward the back of the hall, softly brushing the leaves.

"I thought my feelings for you were finished... Hour after hour, working here at the Temple, hoping to drive the last splinters of you from my heart. Now that you are here with me again, I realize, this was only another way of hardening to the pain I carry. The way you left hurt, Kathrana. Without a goodbye. So casually, matter-of-factly; I woke up that morning and you were gone—"

"We had discussed it, Yama: we were already finished, and had been for some time."

"You turned your back on everything we had been through together," Yama betrayed his anger, flushed at the neck, a stern gesture in his hand.

"I was very clear with you... we were unhappy together."

"But there was so much that was good, there was so much love— what happened to all of that as you walked out of the Inn that morning?"

Kathrana touched Yama's arm— but he recoiled.

"The love was never enough, was it?" Yama averted his eyes, staring deep into the shadowy soils of the garden.

"Yama..." Kathrana, doing her best to speak with control. "Love is not enough to hold two people together."

They stood in heated silence for a while, the call of a Whippoorwill chortling its name in high stillness of the forest. "Why didn't Rowland stop his dogs from killing the Elk?"

"He couldn't have stopped them... Once he made the call, they were triggered to make the kill."

"So a beautiful animal had to die because of his fear?"

Kathrana flashed with anger- "His judgement was not off!" She snapped with a fierce gesture of the hand. "By the next morning it was confirmed without doubt— we were being hunted."

Yama humbled himself, taking a relaxing breath... "Please, continue."

"We put the fires out early that night and slept close. The dogs were lying at the foot of Rowlands bed-mat. The moon was banking over the jagged faces of the mountains. The shadows were full of the singing of frogs growing as the moon's light seeped into the wet pools and bogs surrounding us.

We all lay, listening to the songs, our eyes staring into a starless sky. Gradually, our eyes grew heavy, and one by one, the camp grew silent. Rowland and I were two of the last ones to fall asleep, save two watchmen.

'Rowland, did you see a wraith in the meadow today?' I asked him.

He held the question, his silence weighted in the darkness- 'I have been revisiting the moment all day. I keep playing the scene in my thoughts, confused, doubting my own eyes. I didn't know the Elk was out there. I did not see an Elk, this much, I am certain.'

'Why did you call the attack?'

'I had to respect my judgement in that moment...' he paused, his breathing soft in the shadows.

'And now you question yourself?'

'No...' The singing of the frogs filled the gap between his thoughtful pause. 'But I know fear... and it can take shape in the slightest errors...'

My hand reached for his... 'The watchmen will wake us in a few hours to relieve them...' Rowland squeezed my hand gently. 'You should get some rest.'

I took his arm, and as we rested into the songs of the night, we fell into sleep together.

When I woke, it was already morning, the sun was already breaking through the land. I sat up, surprised. *What happened to my watch?* Rowland wasn't at the camp. A group of the workers were standing in a circle.

'What's going on?' I asked, my cheeks flushed with sleep.

'We lost one of the dogs last night.'

I gasped, "Is it true?'

'Aye… the small male.'

'Archu…' My hand went to my mouth— 'Where is Rowland?'

'Damn creature hung the animal from a tree… Rowland is taking care of the body.'

I was shaken with fright- 'The wraith didn't consume the body?'

'Ney… they devour something deeper…' Dokada's voice grew quiet, his finger tapping his head at the temple- 'They consume something on the inside.'"

Yama retreated, walking across the hall to the open balcony, moonlight slicing across the floor. "The Necro-panther killed Archu…" he said, his body still holding the insecurity of their unresolved conversation. "But how? How did it take Archu without also contending with the other two dogs? If this creature only consumes inside the subconscious of its prey… how did it get close without waking them?"

Kathrana lowered her chin, her eyes closed: "Rowland was concerned about that very same thing. He had been distant the whole next day, steeping in thought, late into the evening…

'No sense sleeping in the dark anymore,' said Dokada as he stopped a man from kicking out the fire. 'The damn devil is already on our trail…'

Rowland was quiet, staring at Kualu and Mincha as they were lying close to his bed.

'Rowland, can I help you?'

He didn't answer, deep in thought.

I thought to let him have his space. The frogs began their nightly songs from the silver muds of the land. The camp quieted, listening, suppressing the fear that was stinging inside everyone. One by one, as sleep overcame fear, the party began to slumber.

I was hearing the nearly mystical symphony of the frogs. My eyes grew heavy in my deepening attention to their songs, filling the night. I pried my eyes open and looked at Rowland. He was fighting for consciousness. I was surprised. He was not a man to succumb, not with the life of his dogs at stake. But I saw him, losing himself to sleep. I noticed the dogs with their massive heads lying over their front paws, their sharpened eyes drooping... I noticed Mincha lift her ears, head heavy, and her irises glistening into a shade of blue. She was looking away into the darkness, her ears turned forward... I was fighting sleep, shaking myself back several times... but the moment before sleep took me completely, I was listening to the musing songs of the night, and a sudden, final thought crossed through my mind— 'The Frogs!'"

Yama was listening now with renewed interest in Kathrana's story- "The song of the frogs were lulling the party to sleep? The Kuwalu were put to sleep too?"

Kathrana nodded- "It was a kind of spell of the Necro-panther... the creature had turned nature against our wills."

Yama paced away from Kathrana, chided, shaking his head- "Similar to love..."

Kathrana suddenly felt compassion for Yama... She remained quiet, observing the lowliness in his posture, the sadness sinking inside him.

"What happened next?"

"The camp was woken to Rowland's cry- 'Kualu!'

I leapt out of my bed. I saw Rowland, still under his blanket, with the huge body of the Kuwadu dog, a corpse lying in his bed.

The camp shuffled into excitement. Some gathering around Rowland's bed-mat.

'We're cursed,' some of them spoke amongst themselves.

Rowland was deeply struck. His hands shook with the pain. I crawled to his side. I wanted to hold him, but I caught myself, remembering I that I was a man to these people... I restrained my affection- 'Kathrana...' he let his words go unspoken, shattered in the turmoil of his grief, lowered his forehead to the body of his companion and wept.

'We're leaving, now. Pack up.' Dokada spoke with immediacy. 'Get a move on! We're two days yet from the sietch. Get yourselves together... Puro...'

I turned to the man, meeting his deep, woody eyes as they fell over me: 'Pack Rowland's gear for him... Rowland, console yourself as quickly as you are able. Take care of your friend. We're moving out as soon as you return.'

Rowland did not linger. We were on our way within the hour, heading northwest toward the shadows of the Witchmold Cliffs. We were heading into new territory. The wastes were giving way to a thickening of trees, richer grounds where vegetation was permitted to grow.

We traveled until late evening and made camp under the cover of forest. We built several fires and held our weapons close. 'We're falling to sleep too easily,' Dokada announced with stern criticism. 'Remember well, gentlemen, we are being hunted—' he allowed the statement to rest amongst us, feeling its weight. Dokada spoke again with strength in the silence that trembled with fear- 'Who here is prepared to meet with the fate of a wraith tonight? Who here has a wish to die in that darkness?'

The team was quiet. No one wished to close their eyes that night— then I remembered the last thought before I succumbed to sleep the previous night: 'It's the frogs!' I said.

'What about them?' Dokada's wooden gaze fell fiercely over me.

'There is something in the song of the frogs that is lulling us to sleep. The dogs too. I came to the realization last night, shortly before Kualu was taken.'

'I am not a man of Mannah,' said Dokada. 'I don't put much stock in magik... But this situation is fucked. These wastes are cursed. I'm inclined to believe you...' He paused, and none dared to breath out until he permitted them to... he gestured to a worker close to him and spoke directly at him- 'Gather cotton from our supplies and create plugs. Everyone must fill their ears. Avoid listening to the sounds of the night. Listen to your breaths, nothing else; not frog or whippoorwill or the breeze in the trees. Gather your wills, men, for your own sakes!'"

"Kathrana—" Yama cut his way into the conversation— emotion swelling inside him: "I must speak my truth..." he spoke with the gentle intensity that was natural to him, dashed with moments of passion. "I can't bare this insecurity another day. I have pivoted my practice on developing the confidence to love myself again... to forgive us for the choices we've made that have lead us to so much resentment, so much pain we've caused each other. But Kathrana, every day that I live here in this Temple, surrounded by the wisdom of the tradition, I am finding no resolution to the difficulty. The day you left, I was broken."

"Yama, we ended it!" Kathrana snapped. "For days we acknowledged the need for it to end."

"Yes, I spoke those words with you…" Yama turned, faced Kathrana with all his courage. "But my heart was in a different place. All I really wanted was to heal things. I spoke those words because I didn't want the problems between us to continue hardening our hearts. I thought, if we had the space to relax the tensions of holding the relationship together, we would soften into love again… and then you left without a care."

"I had to go, Yama."

Yama pulled his eyes away, faced the wide expanse of the mountain slopes diving into darkness-"I fought everyday to put our love above the resentment and the misunderstandings… the way you left disrespected everything I offered to the relationship."

"It was your choice to give, Yama!"

"And it was your choice to *take*!" Yama spun around, throwing his hands up, walking like fire across the courtyard to stand beside the low-burning candles. He paced the length of the altar, Kathrana moving swiftly to his side—

"Get over it, Yama. There is still love between us— I still feel it. This doesn't need to come between us like it is."

"As you said, Kathrana…" Yama gazing into a candle flame. "The love isn't enough."

Yama felt the walls lift around Kathrana. She stepped away and faced the quiet shadows of the garden. They stood in silence a long time, the moonlight angling across the room, the song of a Whippoorwill calling from the treetops.

"You've come here to tell me your story…" Yama spoke sternly. "Please— go on…"

Kathrana took a frustrated breath before recalling where she left-off…

"We all lay on the final night, our ears plugged deeply with cotton, some wrapping cloth around their heads also, suppressing all the sound that they could. Rowland had been silent the entire day. I remained close to him, offering my unspoken support.

As night crept over us, the frogs began to sing, chirp by chirp, croak and chortle, the symphony began to elaborate through the darkening woods.

Despite the cotton plugs, the nightly sounds penetrated. They seemed to sing louder than ever. Their music enveloped the forest, washing through the wills of all the men in the camp, gradually, one by one, succumbing them into sweet slumber.

'You must resist, Kathrana,' Rowland said, his eyes hazy, red and throbbing with sleep. 'Don't listen to them. Evade your listening. Listen within yourself.'

His words spoke to me. I closed my eyes to listen only to the swift beating of my heart. As I settled into the silence within me, I was shaken out of it by the piercing bark as Mincha raised to her feet and faced the deep shadows beyond the firelight, her eyes blue, dazzling and cold.

'It's coming,' said Rowland heavily, slowly. 'Resist the urge, Kathrana.'

The camp was falling silent. A few still stirred, but even as the most will-strong of the men fought to remain conscious, they gradually lay down to the ground, persuaded by the urge to fall deep into unconsciousness.

I was on my knees- 'Rowland, I'm so scared—'

There was no response. I turned to him. He was on the ground.

'No Rowland!' I shook him with all my might, but he couldn't wake.

Mincha's barking grew lethargic. Her eyes, once blue, turned to a stone grey, dull and heavy. She curled behind her tail and settled onto the ground, her eyes, looking up at me, blinking, and finally fading to sleep.

I was alone.

Suddenly a voice spoke through the dark, filling the groggy weight of my mind with a menacing reverb—

'Sleep.' it said to me. A shadow prowled across the edge of the fire, resting again into a seat and staring back into the firelight at me: 'Sleep.'

The urge swept over me. My consciousness drifted. I felt the presence of the Necro-panther encroaching, it was inside my mind, and also, sitting at the edge of the fire—

'Sleep.'

By some will, I snapped awake, found myself sitting behind the fire, my head rocking back and forth. The wraith came into focus again. It was on its feet again, poised forward into the firelight. It had stopped suddenly when I broke out of my sleep.

'You cannot resist.' The creature's voice chided within my thoughts. 'You are weak against me.'

I shook my head, rubbed my hands hard into my eyes and took a deep breath of thick air. 'I will not sleep,' I said.

A thin outline appeared in the darkness and smiled. 'You stay awake for him?'

I did not turn my eyes away, but my thoughts went to Rowland, asleep beside me. The question wicked deep inside me. 'I stay awake for everyone.' I said swiftly, trying not to betray the shake of fear in my body.

The smile widened in the shadows, laughter danced through the forest... 'You are in love.'

My eyes averted into the fire. I couldn't bare the wickedness inside the face that stared from the dark."

Yama suddenly paced over to the veranda. Kathrana cut-off her words and watched him. He leaned and looked up into the moonlight. "Is it true?"

Compassion filled Kathrana. She felt Yama's heart held away from her, kept close in the safety of his distance.

"Yes, Yama... I Love Rowland."

Yama flinched. The pain surprised him. He looked up at the night sky, remembering how, in his years as a young man, he had never seen the immense light of the stars. He sighed- "Please continue."

Kathrana took a breath and let her eyes linger on Yama, seeing his hands gently trembling.

"I thought of you, Yama, in this moment as the wraith spoke of love. A deep swell of confusion arose. The buffalo herds ran in wild sweeps through my heart. I remembered both their beauty and their immense desperation. We were very much like them, weren't we, darling?"

"Yes… we were running, chased by our own faults of love.

"We were not wrong, Yama."

He looked away again… "What happened next?"

"Sleep was burning on my eyes. My heart was collapsing. I stayed my gaze into the flames of the hearth. A voice crept through my ear like a sharp wind: 'You will only become another dog to him, Kathrana.'

The panther shifted to the far right of the camp, sat back, a thin smile in the dancing edges- 'You know… you know I am right.'

I resisted to accept the creature's words. But I couldn't restrain from hearing him speak.

'You are a dog, Kathrana—' the voice shifted around the camp to the left side- 'A wet bitch for service. These are the kind of dogs Rowland pays for…'

I gazed harder into the flames, tears glistening under my eyes.

'He has held your secret… payment is now on his mind… ahhhh, yes, I see it…. he dreams of it now. There you are… lying at his feet during the day. Between his legs in the night… a whore.'

Sleep was fervent in my head. I drifted again. My head wobbled; I snapped upright.

'Ah, there is another... A man you are running from... I see him. Yama. Yama. Such sorrow in a man. You were too weak for him. You even run like a bitch.'

My hands were trembling against the bow and arrow in my grip. My body began to shake. My teeth shivering as they held back the deep sobbing locked in my throat.

'Sleep now... put away this pain... Sleep... Sleep....'

My body filled with the instinct. The trilling of the frogs grew deeper into my mind, the firelight closed around me, my thoughts drifting further into a place of deep, comforting darkness.

Suddenly, in a moment near the horizon-line of unconsciousness, I looked deep into the white tendrils of light singing inside the logs, heat hissing through the flames— I plunged my hand into the fire.

There was an instant searing— burning, scorching. Every fiber of my body became alert and awake. Every ounce of consciousness was involved in the pain. My hand was blistering inside the heat. My body was pain. My heart was pain. But I wouldn't withdrawal— I couldn't. In this moment, death was more real than the trauma of any pain.

The intensity rose up through me. The fluids of my body curdled with agony. I was horrified by myself as fear parted my mouth, my voice poised on a beat of silence, and then— I screamed. It carried throughout the forest, rhythms upon rhythms stopping to shudder at the sound of a woman's pain. Something primal rose from the roots of my body. Horror divided me into pieces of skin and bone, hair and muscle, fluid and tissue... seeing this animal within me, terrified and alone, I screamed even brighter through the woodlands.

Suddenly, Rowland rolled onto his elbow. His eyes opened, his head shaking away the sleep. He immediately saw my arm reaching into the flames and he leapt to pull me out of the fire. Dark red flesh returned smoking from the flames. I held my arm close and recoiled to the ground. Men stirred in the camp. But no other man could wake.

Rowland hurried to his sword and drew a white blade into the firelight. The Necro-panther slid aside into the shadows, reappeared to the right... then the left... his shadow passing around the camp. We heard his laughter through the treetops. Dancing through our minds. Rowland was unmoved. His sword poised against the night.

Suddenly a darkness rolled across the back of the camp, completely dowsing the flames of the furthest hearth. Smoke bellowed across the sleeping caravan. Then, a second fire was swallowed into the shadow. A third hearth trembled and then sank below the heavy weight of blackness. The fire between Rowland and I was all that remained.

A lean figure rushed through the firelight of our hearth. Flames fell apart and spat across the dirt. Rowland's sword struck nimbly through the waving light and grazed the shadow. It retreated outside the camp without dowsing the fire. I quickly threw a fist of kindling into the fire to revive it.

Rowland faced the surrounding night. A silver form prowled behind the wagons. A long inklike dash traveled through the silhouettes of the sleeping camp. I stood with my hand protected close to my chest. My legs shook. I fell down again.

'Stay!' Rowlands hand gestured me down again. I welcomed the ground where I fell. Exhausted, I held my heavy head to the ground.

A voice passed through my mind- 'You see, bitch... already, he is putting you in your place.'

The voice made me tremble— I lowered my forehead in reverence, feeling the comfort of the deep earth.

Bright eyes flashed as the form of a panther ran with full stride into the circle of the hearth. Rowland opened his reach wide, endless black within black of the panther's body clashed against the glitter of Rowlands white sword. The two forces met and a bright light submerged the entire camp. The creature howled and danced across the grounds, prowling to the edge of firelight and then curving around for a fresh attack. Rowland pivoted, dodged the white striking of a paw. The creature remained low, looking up the length of Rowland's body, white sabers flashing inside a black skull.

I stood to my feet, poised with my bow and arrow at hand.

Rowland opened his stance toward the creature- 'Get back! Leave this fireside, devil!'

The mouth of the panther furled open with the mock of laughter- 'What power do you have over me?'

'I possess the power of all men before me,' said Rowland. 'The strength of the living earth below my feet...I *am* power.'

I watched intensely, a deep swell of love rising inside me, I raised my weapon without fear.

The creature laughed and crawled across the ground, setting his gaze deep inside my eyes- 'You cannot save yourself... I will eat the flesh of this man. I will consume you in the depths where you sleep in fear... Your love is not enough.'

Rowland lunged forward to strike. The wraith vanished, resurfacing across the fire and plunging itself through the flames. A plume of sparks rose into the treetops, embers whirled across Rowland's face, and a sudden flash of teeth wrapped themselves around his thigh.

Rowland collapsed to one knee roaring in the pain as the shadow of the Necro-panther leapt out of sight, reapearing in the pith of the night, there was a flash of silver eyes, a sudden parting of the shadows gave way to a grinning face.

Spontaneously I drew back my bow. With stinging flesh, I pulled the tension of the string with my scorched hand, poised the arrow— laughter rippling through the forest, Rowland down on his knees between me and the target, my hand piercing with blisters.

Suddenly, before I recognized what had happened, my fingers slipped in the blood of my wounds. The arrow released prematurely, leapt a swift distance, and impaled—

Rowland dropped to the ground, leaning on one arm, breaths panting with my arrow through his breast.

I froze with terror. My heart sank deep into the sudden grief of my mistake.

The darkness was rolling in laughter- 'Well done, Archer!'

In the same beat, the Necro-panther took shape inside the firelight. I knocked another arrow. My hand stabbing with pain. I pulled the bow taught. The arrow flew through the open shadows and struck the wraith in the pith of his forehead, deep into the empty face of the creature. A white sinew of fluid and searing puss poured forward. A rushing haunt of screams split the darkness.

I ran to Rowland's side and collapsed, overcome with fatigue. His arms reached out to hold me as the fire blew into a flurry of ash and shadows. The light gave way to a sudden stamp of darkness. Laughter shuddering through the treetops as the wraith rippled outward into nothingness— we lay collapsed in the sudden silence... trembling in our embrace."

Dawn was breaking before the view from the temple. Yama and Kathrana stood close as a soft understanding flowed between them, watching the sun breaking over the Wilding Plains.

"Did Rowland survive?" Yama spoke at a near whisper, morning birds stirring along the steep banks.

Kathrana winced below the raw touch of the memory: "He survived until we reached the sietch... he died before the next morning."

Silence lingered between them. "Kathrana— I'm sorry..."

"It's ok, Yama… I wrestled with the grief the rest of my journey. Mincha was my guide through the remaining wilderness between the North Passage to the Pampah Plains. It was like having a part of Rowland with me as I finished my journey. I was grateful to have had her with me. When I arrived to the place of my people, it was the day after the Gwen Eden had passed into the realm of Kenya. I was there for her ceremonial release from the braid of the tribe… It was there that we also released Rowland's spirit to the stars."

"I understand the grief of death, more than any other," said Yama, deep with compassion. "I have seen men die at my own hands. There are no words to relieve the past… however, there is forgiveness. It is organic, unfolding over time. But there is tremendous fault in carrying our mistakes the rest of our lives. This temple and the practices have been the gradual wind that pulls the threads of pain from my heart. I encourage you, Kathrana, to forgive yourself whatever way you can."

"I've faced the grief long enough. When we performed the ritual for his death in my home-village, we lit the fires of his life, and I felt his forgiveness… I was able to forgive myself in turn…" Kathrana turned her eyes to Yama- "Now I am here to find our forgiveness."

Yama held his heart open, a deep breath filling him with love: "I have been fighting my pain for so long… I wanted only to hear you recognize that your actions were painful for me. I do not need your apology. The practice is my own. I only wish to know that you honor the path we've shared, the consequences of our love."

Kathrana softened into her next words: "That is why I am here."

Massive white clouds waded in the blue ribbons of dawn as the east filled with gradual light. A gong rang from the mosque above the village. The lower courtyard was stirring with quiet movement as the Sanyas made their way toward morning meditations.

Kathrana watched the movement of green robes across the clean architecture of earth and stone- "You have found your dream of being a hero on the mountainside, Yama..." Kathrana was smiling, her hand touching Yama's. "You're fighting the war inside you every day from these clifftops."

Yama opened his heart to the remaining moments they shared as the sun rose over them, however brief, however tender, Kathrana took his hand and smiled.

"Will you stay, Kathrana, for a while? You are welcome in this place."

"Thank you, Yama... Soon I must make my way east... what awaits me there, I do not know."

"The road of Depoah Manu calls on you?"

"Yes, I suppose it does." Kathrana's eyes squinted in the brightening light of the morning. "The path has never let me go. I was always guided by it, even as I defied its lessons— will you stay here at the Temple?"

Yama smiled, placing his other hand over hers: "Gradually, Kathrana, I am finding the peace I seek."

Today is for Peace

There is more to understanding

than meeting truth along a foreign road.

There is more to loving

than the face of the person beside you.

Remember, reality grows from pain.

The pond is broken by a fin

emerging from its own deep-water secrets.

We all have to witness

as the world throws stones

and storms cast branches

autumn lets her clothes fall

and the walnuts come home with more than they can

bear.

There is a cycle for everything that breaks

for the sweet oil within itself.

There is a season for building fires

and there is a time for abandoning our house.

Yesterday you might have been drinking

from the damaged pottery of your believing—

tomorrow you might have an empty basket…

But today

today

let there be Peace.

The Archer

Songs of Yama

Joseph Montgomery